Twayne's English Authors Series

Sylvia E. Bowman, *Editor*

INDIANA UNIVERSITY

Hugh Walpole

 **TEAS** *120*

Hugh Walpole

By ELIZABETH STEELE

University of Toledo

Twayne Publishers, Inc.   ::   New York

For My Family and Friends

Preface

There has been no book-length appraisal of Hugh Walpole's work since 1933 when *Hugh Walpole: A Study* by novelist Marguerite Steen appeared. Between that date and his death in 1941, Walpole wrote ten novels, three plays, an autobiography, and many short stories. These works—in which he developed certain latent talents, reacted to current affairs, broadened his audience, and maintained his place as a notable representative of traditional English prose—need and merit now the attention his early fiction received in Miss Steen's study and in *Tradition and Hugh Walpole* by Clemence Dane (1929). Neither of these writers discussed Walpole in his important role of literary critic. Nor was their analysis of his fiction definitive. Their lack of historical perspective and their failure, for whatever reason, to make use of original source materials, are weaknesses the present-day critic can fortunately avoid.

In 1952 Macmillan's published *Hugh Walpole, A Biography* by Rupert Hart-Davis, Walpole's friend and official biographer. Widely recognized for its excellence, it is not a study of his literary work but concentrates instead, deftly and with unstinting detail, on his busy life and host of well-known, interesting friends.

The purpose of my own study is to show the sources of Hugh Walpole's success as a writer during the thirty-five years and fifty books of his career. In that era, when modernists like Virginia Woolf and D. H. Lawrence received increasingly serious attention from critics, novelists like Hugh Walpole continued to appeal to readers on both sides of the Atlantic who preferred that their fiction be traditional. The present study draws parallels between his writings and those of other traditionalists, from the eighteenth century to the twentieth.

Decisions about quality are necessarily mine since the critical consensus about Walpole's work is so uneven. Because he was extremely prolific, the bulk of my study follows what I might call an "organic" pattern: six chapters (II-VII) present the author in certain roles related to his material. One of Walpole's six best-known novels provides the occasion for each chapter, and to this extent the chapters proceed chronologically. The other novels (thirty-two) and the literary criticism are arranged by theme, as designated in the chapter titles, whereas the short stories and the memoirs have a chapter to themselves. Facts about Hugh Walpole's life, so far as they relate to his work, are found throughout the discussion.

My indebtedness for materials is greatest to Sir Rupert Hart-Davis, the London publisher and Walpole's literary executor, who during a fascinating weekend in his Yorkshire home showered me with Walpoliana. I cannot thank him enough for his continued kindness and courtesy. For making other items available, gratitude is due Mrs. Mary M. Hirth, Librarian, Academic Center, University of Texas, and Dr. Lola L. Szladits, Curator of the Henry W. and Albert A. Berg Collection, New York Public Library.

The list of befrienders is long, but it must include Hubert H. Dumville, Yorkshire, long-time admirer and publicist of Walpole; Alex Barber, who directed me to the University of Birmingham for the Brett Young-Walpole letters; Bartholomew C. C. Price of the Toledo Public Library, gracious, tireless and knowledgeable about England; Roger Medill, curator of the Walpole Collection, King's School, Canterbury; Dr. Helmut Gerber, Arizona State University; T. M. Farmiloe, Macmillan's, London; Heather Scott, Doubleday's, New York; Paul Myers, Curator, Theatre Collection, Lincoln Center Library; Dr. Richard M. Ludwig, Princeton University; Dr. Blair Rouse, guardian of the Swinnerton-Walpole letters, University of Arkansas; Mr. and Mrs. Frederick Cook and Mrs. Cook's mother, Mrs. Claire Anyon, present inhabitant of Walpole's house at Polperro, Cornwall; and the library staffs of the British Museum; Oxford and Cambridge universities; Rare Book Room, Library of Congress; Alexander Turnbull Library, Wellington, N. Z.; Arnold Bennett Museum, Burslem, Stoke-on-Trent; Fitzwilliam Museum, Cambridge; National Library of Scotland, Edinburgh, and Northwestern University, Evanston.

Special thanks are due Dr. Sylvia Bowman, dedicated editor of the Twayne English Authors Series; and four friends and mentors at Bowling Green State University: Dr. Richard C. Carpenter, especially; Drs. Lowell Leland, Frank Baldanza, and Stanley Coffman; and Dr. William Thomas, Findlay College.

Preface

To my parents, George and Berniece Smith, beloved Anglophiles; my mother-in-law, Mary Waterman Steele, who understands, and my husband, Arthur R. Steele—my gratitude has no limits.

ELIZABETH STEELE

University of Toledo

Acknowledgments

For permission to quote from letters, diaries, journals and books by Walpole and others, I am grateful to Sir Rupert Hart-Davis, Marske-in-Swaledale, Richmond, Yorkshire; Mrs. Mary M. Hirth and the Manuscript Committee, Academic Center Library, The University of Texas; Macmillan and Company, Ltd., London; and the Henry W. and Albert A. Berg Collection of The New York Public Library, Astor, Lenox and Tilden Foundations.

Contents

Preface

Acknowledgments

Chronology

1. The Position of Hugh Walpole 17
2. Acolyte 26
3. Artist 42
4. Witness 55
5. Evangelist 73
6. Critic 94
7. Romanticist 116
8. Other Fiction, Other Prose 136
9. Review and Perspective 147

Notes and References 153

Selected Bibliography 162

Index 171

Chronology

1884   Hugh Seymour Walpole born March 13, Parnell, Auckland, New Zealand.

1890   Family moved to New York City.

1894– Hugh alone in England at school Marlow, Buckingham-
1898   shire, and King's School, Canterbury.

1898– Family moved to Durham; Hugh in Durham School; wrote
1902   juvenilia.

1903– In Cambridge. Autumn 1905, first published work, critical
1905   essay "Two Meredithian Heroines," *Emmanuel College Magazine*.

1906   Bachelor's degree, history. Lay Missioner, Mersey Mission to Seamen, Liverpool.

1907   April-July, tutored children of famous author "Elizabeth" (then Gräfin von Arnim), Germany.

1908   Taught French, Epsom College, Surrey.

1909   Plunged into London literary life. May, *The Wooden Horse*, first published novel.

1910   *Maradick at Forty*. First published short story, "Giving Up," *Smart Set*.

1911– *Mr. Perrin and Mr. Traill* (*The Gods and Mr. Perrin* in
1913   America). *The Prelude to Adventure*. *Fortitude*.

1914– *The Duchess of Wrexe*. World War I began; rejected for
1915   poor eyesight, served in Russia as Red Cross Sanitar, Carpathians; awarded St. George's Cross. *The Golden Scarecrow*.

1916– *The Dark Forest*. *Joseph Conrad*. Head, Anglo-Russian
1917   Propaganda Bureau, Petrograd.

1918   Made Commander of the Order of the British Empire. *The Green Mirror*. In Russian section, Ministry of Information, London.

1919– *The Secret City. Jeremy.* September-April, first American
1920　lecture tour. *The Captives.*

1921　*The Thirteen Travellers. The Young Enchanted.*

1922– September-June, second American lecture tour. *The Cathe-*
1923　*dral.* Awarded Doctor of Laws degree, Tufts College.
　　Jeremy and Hamlet.

1924– *The Old Ladies. The Crystal Box. Portrait of a Man with*
1925　*Red Hair.*

1926– *Harmer John.* October-April, third American lecture tour.
1927　*Jeremy at Crale.*

1928　*Wintersmoon. Anthony Trollope. The Silver Thorn.*

1929– *Farthing Hall* (with J. B. Priestley). *Hans Frost.* December-
1930　March, fourth American lecture tour. *Rogue Herries.*

1931　Dramatized *The Cathedral* (play opened November 1932,
　　published 1937). *Above the Dark Circus* (*Above the Dark
　　Tumult* in America). *Judith Paris.*

1932– *The Fortress. The Apple Trees. All Souls' Night. Va-*
1933　*nessa.*

1934　June-December, in Hollywood. *Captain Nicholas.*

1935– August-June, in Hollywood. *The Inquisitor. A Prayer for*
1936　*My Son.* October-December, 1936, fifth (final) American
　　lecture tour.

1937　Knighted. *John Cornelius. The Haxtons* (play, opened Janu-
　　ary 19, 1939, published 1939).

1938　*Head in Green Bronze. The Joyful Delaneys.*

1939– World War II began. *The Sea Tower. Roman Fountain.*
1940　*The Bright Pavilions.*

1941　June 1, died at home, Brackenburn; buried in St. John's
　　churchyard, Keswick, Cumberland. *The Blind Man's House*
　　(posth.).

1942– *The Killer and the Slain. Katherine Christian. Mr. Huf-*
1948　*fam.*

CHAPTER 1

The Position of Hugh Walpole

I Public Testimony

"WHO'S Hugh?" asked the New York *Sun* rhetorically in 1919, introducing Hugh Walpole, the man destined to become the best-known contemporary British writer in America during the next two decades. Any literate American could answer the question by 1929; and, by 1939, the face of Sir Hugh Walpole, the stalwart of English fiction, was so familiar that a theater critic protested his brief appearance in the movie *David Copperfield*, claiming that audiences would recognize him and be distracted from the story.[1] Yet after his death during World War II, Walpole's name dropped suddenly from sight. His literary repute suffered, seemingly, from the lack of his personal presence; and the eclipse has deepened with the passing years until "Who's Hugh?" is again a legitimate query. When today's young teachers of literature confuse Sir Hugh Walpole (1884–1941) with his ancestral cousin Horace Walpole (1717–97), fourth Earl of Orford, the error is almost understandable.

Yet many older, nonacademic readers have never heard of the fourth Earl of Orford, while the name "Hugh Walpole" recalls memories of faithfully buying and sharing his books, naming their children and dogs after children and dogs in them—tributes appropriate to a novelist popular in England and in America with the cultivated "middlebrow" public. To a reading generation who were familiar with the great British traditionalists Walter Scott, Charles Dickens, William M. Thackeray, and Rudyard Kipling, and who admired Washington Irving more than Henry James, and Robert Louis Stevenson more than Joseph Conrad, the "new" British novel after 1914 was something of a challenge. Because Virginia Woolf and James Joyce, glimpsed in magazine excerpts and brief book reviews, were communicating in unaccustomed ways, they seemed not to communicate at all. D. H. Lawrence was plainer, but his subject matter was all too plain; and he distressed readers unused to earthy sexuality in fiction.

Fortunately for such readers, not all writers were taking these new directions. Until his death in 1931, Arnold Bennett continued to present detailed, sometimes grim, sometimes light, journalistic slices of life. During a creative period almost as long, John Galsworthy continued to document in his Forsyte novels the English upper middle class, past and present, in an often ironic but always compassionate light. For the more sophisticated, there was Somerset Maugham, who was the traditionalist's Lawrence. Upon these three—Bennett, Galsworthy, and Maugham—contemporary in content and conventional in approach, the tradition-loving reader could always depend. But, because writers are mortal, it was also reassuring to find some dozen younger novelists,[2] of the same age as Mrs. Woolf, Joyce, and Lawrence, who still kept to the noble mainstream of English fiction. Of these younger traditionalists Hugh Walpole became the best known by virtue of his talents, his hard work, and a certain penchant for publicity.

Timeliness and publishers were other helpful factors. He was fortunate enough to be in Russia before and during the 1917 Revolution, and two of his better novels resulted from the experience. In 1930 he launched his well-known historical novels, the Herries series, just before the Depression made long "costume romances" popular with readers again. His publishers too were excellent aides—Smith Elder, his first, an old respected company who had published Jane Austen and Thackeray; Martin Secker, a young publisher with fine tastes, idealistic and interested in new writers; and, finally, Macmillan's, one of the world's best-known firms. In America, after a brief contract with Century Company, he went to George Doran's, who later merged with Doubleday.

On the surface Walpole's life, in fact, was full of good fortune. His hard-working, brilliant father was descended from England's first prime minister. His modest, charming mother numbered among her ancestors government officials and professional men—doctors, lawyers, teachers. There was a famous writer on each side of the family: Horace Walpole and Richard Harris Barham (better known in England than America), author of the *Ingoldsby Legends*. Hugh's education in private schools and at Cambridge, followed by a tour of France and Germany during which he

[18]

stayed in private homes to learn the language—all befitted a gentleman's son. In his job as tutor to author "Elizabeth's" children in Germany, he had been preceded by E. M. Forster, himself now a novelist of reputation.

When, after halfhearted attempts at teaching and missionary work, Walpole plunged at last into literary life, he promptly made friends with Henry James, Arnold Bennett, H. G. Wells, and half a dozen lesser authors. Touched by the young man's attentions, they were glad to help this ebullient, attractive son of the new Bishop of Edinburgh. He repaid their efforts not only with deference but with unceasing energy on his own behalf, coupled with modesty. Moreover, he was good-looking, dressed well, and had an excellent speaking voice.

Later travels took him throughout Europe and North America and as far south as Egypt. With proceeds from his writing and lectures, he amassed an outstanding art collection. He learned to appreciate music, and became the chief backer of Lauritz Melchior, the famous Wagnerian *Heldentenor*. He encouraged and gave solid financial help to countless authors, minor and major. He started the Society of Bookmen, still a flourishing organization of publishers, booksellers, and writers. As more than passing acquaintances he knew Queen Mary and Mary Pickford, Adolf Hitler and Charlie Chaplin, Gene Tunney and Ernest Hemingway, and hundreds of others.

Yet Hugh Walpole's life was not all success and happiness. In his autobiographies, which are frank, we see a young boy in school situations abhorrent to him—not the first nor last time such a story has been told in fact and fiction. Classmates in the dormitories, when they discovered his sensitive nature, taunted him; masters in the classroom, before his severe myopia was discovered, sneered at him for being stupid. During these years his parents were in New York, thousands of miles away. When they returned, it was to take Hugh away from his best school so far, King's at Canterbury, and to enroll him as a lowly day student at Durham School in the North Country town of Durham.

Despite Hugh's later defense of his parents and the world's praise of Bishop Walpole, we wonder about the relations between the Bishop and his wife. Clearly, they failed to provide an example of wedded bliss: none of their three children married. Hugh describes his father as preoccupied and tireless, a "saint" who "did not really understand evil"; and his mother (who had been partially deaf since childhood) as combining diffidence with a strong streak of sarcasm. Hugh's energy and optimism were his father's; his wit, perhaps his mother's; but he had a need for demonstrative affection which neither parent seemed able to provide. One result was their son's lifelong doubt about how relationships between the sexes could or should be conducted—a doubt that caused him perpetual tension.

Thus, we see the two sides of Hugh Walpole's personal experience, the light and the dark, the dark perhaps seeming darker because of the brightness of the light. Himself aware of the dichotomy, at times he felt almost torn apart by it. The reader seeking explanations for the unevenness of Walpole's work, does well to remember it also.

II *Professional Opinion*

On October 12, 1931, Walpole in his journal wrote of certain fellow authors that "It is my contemporaries who will not say a word for my work. Arnold [Bennett], Swinnerton, . . . Maugham . . . —these have been my 'downers' and my critics—not the younger generation who, like Priestley, . . . Marguerite Steen, . . . [L. A. G.] Strong help me on every side. Of course I am Romantic and [my] whole generation has been against Romanticism . . . but there is also some jealousy I think." Then a few lines later he admitted: "If they thought me good enough they wouldn't be jealous."

His comments tell the story well, but not the whole story. Early in Walpole's career he was mentioned favorably, along with others, by Henry James, in a *Times Literary Supplement* article, entitled "The Younger Generation." [3] Unfortunately, James was a personal friend of the young writers he praised; and the fact that the same article described D. H. Lawrence and E. M. Forster as unworthy hardly endeared Walpole and his favored fellows to contemporary proponents of the New Novel: Virginia Woolf, Forster himself, Katherine Mansfield, T. S. Eliot, Dorothy Richardson, Lytton Strachey, and John Middleton Murry. These British practitioners of the so-called Modern School, whose craft derived from Continental poetry, criticism, and fiction, called themselves "Georgians" after the reigning monarch George V (r. 1910–1936). Their quarrel with the mainstream of English fiction—overrun, they felt, by Edwardians like H. G. Wells, Arnold Bennett, and John Galsworthy—[4]was that it was stagnant. The Georgians intended to freshen it.

Indeed, it is clear today that they did; and Walpole, despite many misgivings (see Chapter 6), was among those who paid tribute to their work. But he could not ignore the fact that he himself, though temporally one with the Georgians, was temperamentally an Edwardian, in his writings at least. One of his talents, for instance, was creating plots. As practiced by James Joyce, Virginia Woolf, and Katherine Mansfield, the New Fiction deprecated plot. Mrs. Woolf, especially, scorned Galsworthy, Bennett, and Wells as timid slaves "constrained . . . by some powerful and unscrupulous tyrant," presumably the conventional reader, "to provide a plot." [5] She said nothing publicly about Hugh Walpole; and his official biographer, Rupert Hart-Davis, states that "She was one of the few people who accepted him at his own valuation as a 'real abnormal romantic' and he gratefully and delightedly responded." [6]

Other feminine writers of his own generation, Katherine Mansfield and Rebecca West, did not let him escape so easily. Later, he became a target for Elizabeth Bowen, V. S. Pritchett, and Graham Greene, novelist-critics younger than himself. Their well-founded comments, far from vindictive, negatively affected his reputation among highbrows; yet they continued to read and review his work. The middlebrows in Britain, America, and Europe, where his novels were widely translated, enjoyed him unabatedly. Biographies of him were published in 1929 and 1933; both were laudatory and both, it should be noted, were written by younger novelists.

When in 1952 the fine official biography by Rupert Hart-Davis was published and received unanimous praise, most reviewers used the occasion to ask, "As a novelist was Hugh Walpole really important or not?" Their consensus was that, although he had been, in 1952 he was not. During the last two decades, however, some of his fiction has made minor news as drama on the stage, on the movie screen, and on television. A recent check in a big-city American library indicates that his works still circulate; [7] and, when Harvard University opened its Lamont undergraduate library in 1949, seven of the one hundred thousand volumes specially selected—three of nonfiction and four novels—were by

Hugh Walpole.[8] *Books in Print* lists twelve Walpole hardback titles (most published by English firms). Translations also continue to be made, including Arabic, Turkish, Icelandic, and Urdu. Occasional essays and short stories appear in anthologies. One, *The Unhumans*, a collection of macabres, can be found on American drugstore racks; and the paperback edition of *Dr. Doolittle*, issued concurrently with the movie, contains an "after-word" written forty years ago by Hugh Walpole.

III *Foundation in Tradition*

That Walpole as a writer was once better thought of than he is today is not a sufficient reason for studying him, and my purpose in writing about him is not to prove that he is a forgotten genius. But his former popularity is an interesting fact of literary history and to pinpoint its "why" may be helpful. Before concentrating on specific works, let us consider some reasons for his popular appeal. To begin with, he represented something well beloved and indubitably valuable—the English novel in the grand tradition. Not that he was of Charles Dickens', George Eliot's, or Thomas Hardy's caliber, but his art had deep roots. It rested strongly on the past while welcoming the present, and it never hurried toward the future.

Although known best as a novelist, Walpole was also a true "man of letters." He wrote countless prefaces for other people's books and thirty for his own Cumberland Edition; he conducted book columns for some half-dozen periodicals, English and American; [9] he edited several anthologies, including one from his own novels; he wrote all or part of six movie scenarios,[10] and composed scores of public lectures and radio talks. His permanent bibliography contains five plays, six works of literary criticism, and five of autobiography—besides one hundred and five short stories and thirty-six novels. Such creative energy was a facet of the grand old tradition; and, if quantity affected quality, as of course it did, this chance was one that writers in that tradition took. Walpole's fecundity came about naturally, not only from the example of older novelists—Fielding, Dickens, Trollope, names that *are* the English novel—and not only because it was the way he earned his living, but because, of the many things in life he enjoyed, writing was first. The aura of youth and enthusiasm that his works exude is their most consistent feature and one of their most attractive.

The loose structure of most of his stories—one or more subplots, many characters and events, and much physical detail—also follows tradition. Discursiveness was an asset especially to serial writers like Thackeray, Trollope, Dickens, and Kipling (and scores of lesser names). Walpole himself seldom wrote for serialization, but most of the works he had read as a boy emerged in that form through the magazines of the day. He absorbed their manner as he absorbed food and drink, with at least two results. One is his proclivity for ending chapters at their most climactic point. A more unfortunate one, traceable to the same influence, is recapitulation —rehearsing facts the reader already knows—a galling habit outside the installment tale.

His emphasis on setting also reflects tradition. A strong believer in environment, Walpole portrays "place" both geographically and psychologically, with varying mixtures between. His villages invite comparison with Oliver Goldsmith's and Trollope's; his London owes something to George Gissing's realism and even more to Dickens' humanity. His "bizarres," murky macabres with psychotic overtones, remind us again of Dickens or, even more, of the Brontës and of his own ancestor, Horace Walpole.

A sense of ease in the background, meanwhile, cushions the startling events in the foreground. He writes chiefly about England, the country he knew best, and about the upper middle class he belonged to. His male characters are members of the professions, or they live off ample incomes without working. Except one or two private secretaries, his women characters live at home and have servants.

In the area of psychology Walpole does not use types—black is not always black, white not always white—but it is easy to pick out his protagonists and antagonists, "heroes" (or "heroines") and "villains." Underlying his plots is an assumption that the hero or heroine will progress, be better at the end than at the beginning. And the forces bringing this improvement about, if not always external, are at least ascertainable. But this does not imply that they are always Realistic: fears and triumphs often arise from causes we might call "sensational." Historian Frank Mott, for instance, defines literary sensationalism as "emotional excitement produced by extreme means, such as definite emphasis on horrors, murder, extreme violence, irregular sex relations, or extraordinary adventures." Besides "the devious intrigues of Quasimodo in Hugo's *Notre Dame*" and "the whipping to death of Uncle Tom . . . it is very common in early religious books. The tortures of Protestants in Fox's *Book of Martyrs* are extremely sensational." "Such things may be morbid and unwholesome," his definition continues, or "they may stir one's deepest and finest feelings." [11] In Hugh Walpole's fiction, sensationalism is nearly as frequent and as tangible as the aura of youth and gusto. Some of the works are more bizarre than others; but in every Walpole novel there occurs at least one scene like those described by Mott. From childhood Walpole was quick to seize on the unusual, turn it over in his imagination, and build it into the malevolent. Such fancies haunted him even in his sleep. The head of his first boarding school noted "Hugh's nightmares"; and, even as a man, Walpole wrote in his diary, "My dreams are a *curse*." [12] His over-active imagination contributed to his creative eagerness. At the same time, that eagerness must be held responsible for at least two flaws in his writing unmentioned so far: vague thinking and careless writing.

The vagueness is more obvious in his nonfiction, especially in his literary criticism, than in his fiction; yet what are we to make of a metaphor like this in *Vanessa:* "The cry of the gulls made the lazy sky lazier"? And of gratuitous philosophical clots like this from *John Cornelius?* "We look at ourselves in a mirror as though we were reflections of ourselves. There *is* the reality somewhere to give us that reflection, but *where* is the reality?—and as we are, all of us, posturing before mirrors at one and the same time, we destroy one another's chances—for reality can be found only when we are completely and *[sic]* in isolation ourselves. In our anger and disappointment we break the glass of our mirror and are surprised that even the reflection is gone."

Vague thinking is hard to distinguish from careless writing, which in Walpole's case often involves similes. Even in his best novel, *Rogue Herries,* we find an occasional sentence like this one: "The sense of drama, of events that happened always just out of sight, began to bewilder him as though he were beginning to be asked to look in many different directions at once." The poorer novels contain frequent examples, like this one from *The Duchess of Wrexe:* "And yet was not this readiness on his part to forgive

[24]

her sprung from his conviction that she would have told him had she had so much to confess to him?" Clearly an awkward question, especially for the reader! Akin to stylistic carelessness is carelessness over facts, small in themselves perhaps but cumulative in effect. Mrs. Nix has brown hair in *Thirteen Travellers* until, eight pages later, it is "bright yellow" without benefit of tint. Jimmy Bain in *Jeremy* is Johnny Bain four lines later, and so on. Editors too are at fault in these cases; but, wherever the blame lies, many such slips mar a book.

Walpole's strengths, on the other hand, are narrative pace, strong atmosphere, and ingenious twists of plot. Narrative pace involves more action than analysis—moments of tension along the way, some pauses for reflection, with a steady climb toward the climax. Least satisfactory in this respect are Walpole's "Jamesian" novels: *The Duchess of Wrexe* and *The Green Mirror*. Novels that are particularly strong in atmosphere—physical settings that appeal to the reader esthetically or emotionally—include the Russian tales (*The Dark Forest* and *The Secret City*) and, although weak in other ways, *The Inquisitor*.

Ingenious plots are too frequent to number. The "Imaginative Child" in *Head in Green Bronze* turns out to be a transmigrated soul in communication with a dowager countess; God appears on a football field in *Prelude to Adventure;* an awesome headmaster accepts graciously Perrin's heretical outburst against the school in *The Gods and Mr. Perrin;* a murderer becomes the man he has murdered in *The Killer and the Slain*. Various lighthearted twists add ebullience to diversions like *The Joyful Delaneys*, while the only salvation of the very slow *Green Mirror* lies in the delayed but effective rebellions of three seemingly passionless youths.

In the traditional English novel, storytelling is basic. Narrative pace, suspense, atmosphere, ingenious plots, and memorable characters (redhaired Judith Paris and Maude Penethen, Canon Ronder and his bitter opponent Archdeacon Brandon, gypsy-like Agatha Payne, miserly Stephen Furze, virile Dr. Semyonov, adolescent Henry Trenchard, Hamlet the dog, old Mrs. Talland, two-year-old Humphrey Poole—to list a dozen) contribute to good storytelling. Although Hugh Walpole had his faults, he had his superior talents also.

CHAPTER 2

Acolyte

I *The Juvenilia*

WHEN Walpole, age twenty-four, arrived in London in 1909 impatient to begin his professional career, he had been writing novels for over a decade. "When I was fourteen in Wiltshire," he recalled years later (Journal, August 28, 1938), "I would sit . . . in the rectory water-closet spinning out, by the guttering candle, new chapters of the endless 'Arnado the Fearless.' " "Arnado" was not the only historical romance he wrote during adolescence; the Walpole files at the University of Texas contain fourteen such manuscripts with suggestive titles like "For the Sake of the King," "Chronicles of a Lady of Charles I," "In the Days of Queen Mary," and "True and Brave." [1] These early efforts followed the lineage of Sir Walter Scott and more recent historical romancers, Bulwer-Lytton, G. P. R. James, and Marion Crawford, whom he admired and read in magazines like *The Cornhill* and *Blackwood's;* but the young would-be author did his own research.[2] His last effort, written before he left for college in 1903, was "Ornod, the Viking or Pabo, the Monk."

Meanwhile, he had not ignored Realism. He preferred Romance, but the literary magazine he conceived in 1898, with his sister Dorothy as illustrator, demanded more varied fare. Strictly for domestic consumption, the "Social Monthly" (variously called the "Social Miscellany" or "Social Fortnightly") [3] displayed a bewildering set of pseudonyms for Hugh Seymour Walpole. Most of the verse was by "Carrots" (throughout his life, Walpole's personal rubric was a sketched rabbit); [4] stories about children with a moral appended were by "Gaskell," after the popular woman writer; "HAH" wrote Stevensonian serials like "The Carse-stone" (concerning which the editor remarked, it "disapoints [*sic*] us, and is not nearly as good as we had hoped it would be"); "G. S. Winter" wrote "Pastoral," a serial with a Richardsonian plot

("I hope our readers will like the idea of a Synopsis at the beginning of Pastoral; I did it because one of our readers [probably his young brother, Robin] expressed a doubt that he might get 'muddled' "). There were also "Social Chatter," a column by "Uncle George" (Dr. Walpole's first name), and literary criticism by the cabalistic "Zoroaster"—more pseudonyms for the indefatigable Hugh. Such diversity forced him beyond the bounds of historical romance and, with Gaskell and Richardson as his guides, into the rich field of English Realism.

Like most college students, Walpole had little time for writing while he was at Cambridge. His files at the University of Texas contain three literary essays and two short stories from this period.[5] One of the essays, in fact, "Two Meredithian Heroines," published in the *Emmanuel College Magazine*, 1905, was his first published work. The stories, "Fear's Face" and "The Scarlet Fool," show the influence of two American authors, Nathaniel Hawthorne and Edgar Allan Poe, respectively. They indicate young Walpole's continuing interest in the macabre, which had already appeared in his juvenilia under titles like "Phantom Footsteps," by "XYZ."

After graduation, Walpole, determined still to be a professional author, sought more and more in his writing to wed Romanticism with Realism. The uncompleted "Green Courts" (1906) is as much literary criticism as fiction; but "The Abbey" (1906–07), though also incomplete, is a fully conceived novel with two plot strands. The main one is Realistic, concerning a young churchman newly arrived in Rotherlie who encounters administrative problems. The Romantic subplot concerns Kendall, a Rotherlie librarian "of artistic temperament" haunted by his past. Some elements in Kendall's story foreshadow Walpole's well-known novel, *Fortitude* (1913); the main plot reappears, in more serious form, in his famous *Cathedral* (1922). The overall structure of "The Abbey" with its two plot lines, one basically Realistic and the other basically Romantic, attracted Walpole periodically throughout his career, beginning with *Maradick at Forty* (1910). Often, as we shall see, its complexity proved too much for him.

"Troy Hanneton" (1907), completed but never published,[6] is almost wholly Realistic. Although Troy's experiences at home and at school foreshadow Peter Westcott's in *Fortitude*, the tone of the earlier tale is more matter-of-fact. Its Realism and the name

"Troy" lead directly to the young author's next effort, *The Wooden Horse,* his first published novel.

II The Wooden Horse

If, as some have thought, *The Wooden Horse* (1909) seems unusually mature for a first novel, this quality is attributable to two factors: the young author's long apprenticeship, and his having submitted the manuscript to three professional writers for suggestions. He began *The Wooden Horse* in France while en route home from the aristocratic German household of Australian-born novelist "Elizabeth." As noted before, one of his predecessors as tutor of her small daughters was the English writer E. M. Forster, who had published three novels since then. Once back in England, Walpole, drawn to him perhaps by their common experience in Elizabeth's turbulent menage, sent Forster the completed manuscript of *The Wooden Horse.* He also requested assistance from two friends, popular authors of the day, Ethel Colburn Mayne and Charles Marriott. When help came from all three, he gratefully accepted it. It was a matter of pride—he was determined to succeed as a writer, a career he had chosen over family protests. When *The Wooden Horse* was accepted by the first publisher to whom it was submitted, he was delighted.

The novel opens with a somewhat poignant one-sentence paragraph: "Robin Trojan was waiting for his father." (We realize soon that Robin is the deuteragonist, or second most important character in the story, and that Harry Trojan, the father, is the main character or protagonist.) Twenty years before, Sir Jeremy Trojan had sent his oldest son, a romantic, dreamy lad, to New Zealand to make his fortune. He married there; and, when his wife died, Harry, with the same obtuseness that had led his own father to send *him* away, shipped two-year-old Robin back to the ancestral home in Pendragon, to live with his grandfather, aunt, and uncle.

When Harry returns to Cornwall, his problem is to regain the family's love, especially Robin's, after twenty years of absence. It isn't easy. Sir Jeremy accepts him; but the rest of the family, including Robin, who is the apple of his aunt's eye, disapproves of Harry's breezy New Zealand manners and casual clothes. And, since he is now a successful businessman, the family is amazed and disappointed when he refuses to help Pendragon convert its picturesque old section, the "Cove," into a tourist attraction be-cause he, for nostalgic reasons, likes it as it is. The family's dismay is compounded when he falls in love with Mary Bethel, whose father, a ne'er-do-well bohemian, is a frequenter of the Cove.

Robin is home on vacation from Cambridge where, unknown to his family, he is semi-engaged to a girl of lower-class back-ground. She and her mother now move to Pendragon, but the girl, while willing to break their engagement, refuses to return his love letters, and he fears blackmail. The climax of the novel comes when Harry retrieves the letters, a retrieval which the aunt and uncle are unable to effect, and Robin is thereby reconciled to his father. In the end, Sir Jeremy dies; and the aunt and uncle leave the family mansion in the possession of Harry, his new wife, and Robin.

The theme of *The Wooden Horse* concerns an important socio-economic issue for its time and place: the British law of primogen-iture. As such, the message is aimed at Harry. "To be born an oldest son," the author seems to say, "is not enough: the head of a family must prove his right to the position." Harry establishes his right to the privileges of primogeniture, first, by proving that he can support himself (his brother lives off Sir Jeremy); second, by receiving his father's blessing before the old man dies; third, by making peace with his own son through an act of chivalry: whereas Robin's aunt tries to overawe his girl friend into releasing his letters and his uncle tries to bribe her, it is Harry's kindness and modesty that win her.

Fourth and finally, we are led to believe that the plans Harry and his bride have for the Cove, a compromise between the ag-gressive commercialism of Pendragon's citizens and Harry's own stubborn nostalgia, will benefit the entire town. Analysts of the novel have questioned the attitude within the family. To the critic in the *Athenaeum*, the Trojans' "progressive, even radical tenden-cies where the picturesque village at their feet is concerned, suggest rather a self-made suburban family than a . . . stock of incalculably ancient lineage and prejudices." Another critic felt that since the Trojans were Pendragon's "noble house" and since Harry would be its head when Sir Jeremy died, the townspeople would side with him about the Cove rather than with the rest of his family when he had made his feelings known.[7] But such arguments ignore the heroic convention that Walpole is using, namely, that, in order to win his prize (in this case, his birthright as head of the family), Harry must perform heroic deeds. A virtual stranger to Pendragon after twenty years, he at first arouses antagonism— a societal truism observable throughout the centuries. The author's task is to keep the antagonism alive until Harry has had a chance to perform his deeds of heroism. True, Walpole may have erred in making Harry's public problem the modernization of the Cove.

Walpole never boosted his first novel as he did some of the later ones. "So *mild* a book," he complained of it (Cumberland Preface, ix).[8] But *The Wooden Horse* is not bad. Seldom jejune, it is alert to human foibles; is often witty; and, except for a recapitulative monologue by Robin near the end (the confessional device that mars some of Walpole's later books also), is fairly well paced. Yet I would not suggest a new reprint: even in Britain, primogeniture is no longer a serious problem except in the royal family; and *The Wooden Horse* is not impressive enough in other ways to survive its out-of-date theme.

III   Maradick at Forty

Few passages in *Maradick at Forty* (1910) impress today's reader as being modern in their appeal while still in good taste. Among those few are the love scenes between the protagonist and his proximate inamorata, Mrs. Milly Lester. Sincere, tender, yet realistically incisive, they remained unequaled by Walpole until *Harmer John* sixteen years later. His failure meanwhile to compose moving love scenes for his protagonists was one of several results, some bad, some good, of the mixed critical reception accorded *Maradick at Forty*. The mildly approving reaction to *The Wooden Horse* had emboldened the young author, who knew that he was putting even more energy, more time, into his second novel than he did into his first.

Unlike *The Wooden Horse*, it was not mailed to other writers for help; otherwise, it might have emerged as a better work. Comments like this one, for instance, by Henry James—"The whole thing is a monument to . . . the absence of a plan of composition, alternation, distribution, structure, . . . —so that *line* . . . is replaced by a vast formless featherbediness—"[9] had they reached the author before publication instead of after, would probably have been heeded. Not all criticism of *Maradick* was unfavorable; but those critics he cared most about—James, the *Times Literary Supplement,* the *Spectator,* and his father—disliked the book.[10]

For our purposes, the *Times* review is especially interesting. Bemused like James by the lack of "plan," the reviewer described the novel as "an ambitious attempt to do at least two things at once. . . . The soul-history or heart-history of Mr. Maradick [is] presented literally . . . entangled with character-drawing and hints at nature-worship and satire on suburban manners. . . ." The history of young Tony Gale on the other hand, he thought, inexplicably mixed "comedy" with "melodrama." "The worst of all this is that we do not know how far we are invited to take it seriously." A good question—to which the reviewer's own choice of terms suggests the answer. On the whole, the main plot with its protagonist, James Maradick, is meant "seriously"; the subplot, centering around Tony Gale, is not. Granting this intent, the reader still finds it hard to shift attitudes with every other chapter or sometimes with every other page. If the main plot were the subplot—if Walpole had had the courage to switch them, thereby making the main plot entirely Romantic with Gale as the protagonist—the subplot could have withstood Maradick's careenings between fact and fantasy, satire and melodrama. (A decade later with *The Young Enchanted,* Walpole made this improvement.)

Meanwhile, the reviews of *Maradick at Forty* staggered him; and, for the rest of his career, both privately and publicly, he gave the novel the shortest shrift of all his works. Neither he nor his critics pointed out what to me is its most interesting aspect—one that explains, while it does not excuse, the awkward mixture of comedy, melodrama, and "nature worship" in *Maradick:* the similarities between the novel and Shakespeare's *The Tempest.* The magnitude of what Walpole attempted, makes it easier to understand his dismay at its reception. Without pursuing every parallel, I think I can convince the reader of Walpole's resourcefulness and sense of fun.

In a Cornish seacoast resort (representing the "mysterious western land" of *The Tempest*) Tony Gale, with his Italian first name (the characters in *The Tempest* are Italian) and his titled father (Shakespeare's young man, Ferdinand, is a prince), meets Janet Morelli (Miranda in the play), a young innocent, boyish in her directness.[11] Janet's father, though, is no Prospero; a figure so strong would have overshadowed the protagonist-hero James Maradick (whose closest parallel in the play is Gonzalo, Ferdinand's adviser). Morelli is less intellectual and far less omniscient than the wizard Prospero. Rather, he is an amalgam of two of Prospero's agents, gross Caliban and tricky Ariel. Like Ariel with his pipe, Morelli attracts wild young creatures by playing his flute; but, when they creep to him entranced, he becomes Caliban, wringing their necks and tearing their flesh.

After Janet and Tony elope, Morelli—thwarted in his plan to promote an earthier relationship between the two—attacks Maradick, who helped them escape. The unsavory struggle covers two pages, of which a few sentences will give the flavor: "His hand hung for an instant above Maradick in the air, then it fastened on his arm. . . . One hand was about his neck, but the other had crept in through his shirt and had touched the skin. . . . Then the fingers began to pinch. They caught the flesh and seemed to tear it; it was like knives. . . . [Maradick's] mouth was against Morelli's neck. He had a sudden wild impulse to bite. . . . Then he felt in his neck teeth; something was biting him. . . ."

Despite the sexual implications, even these details have analogs in *The Tempest*. Pinches, whips, and bites are Caliban's daily lot under the discipline of Prospero, who does not, however, administer them. They are meted out by lesser "spirits," and we only hear about them from Caliban. Putting such acts "on stage," so to speak, makes them less real. The purpose, in the plot, of the encounter—to rid Maradick of his lecherous, Caliban-like interest in Mrs. Lester through transferral—is psychologically defensible, but is overwhelmed here by physical detail.

Act IV of *The Tempest* includes a dance between "nymphs and reapers." *Maradick* too has its dance: Treliss' annual romp, which happens to occur the night Maradick arrives at the hotel with his wife and small daughters. After dinner he accompanies Tony, whom he has just met but who is restless and eager to escape the family circle, down to the village. Wild gaiety abounds, and the two men are caught up in "The Dance Around the Town." A sort of daisy-chain tarantella, the dance in its whirling progress ignores all differences of class, age, and sex ("nymphs and reapers"). Participating unwillingly at first, but finally with abandon, Tony and Maradick are initiated into the Order of the *Admonitus Locorum*, the "Spirit of the Place" (an abstraction represented in *The Tempest* by Prospero's court). That this Order exists and has power is the theme of the novel. After the dance, they wander dazedly into an inn, where they meet Andreas Morelli for the first time, with the ensuing complications noted above.

Walpole's most ingenious echo from *The Tempest* involves an odd stage direction in Act IV: "Enter divers Spirits in shape of dogs and hounds, and hunt them about, Prospero and Ariel setting them on." A traveling puppeteer in the novel, Punch, a friend of Tony and Maradick and an enemy of Morelli, has a white dog. Angry at the little man's meddling, Morelli kills his dog, whose spirit then trails Punch and Maradick as they stumble back to town through the fog: "And indeed, in the gathering and shifting mist that went and came and took form and shape, there might have been a thousand white dogs wandering, an army of dogs. . . . One new dog had joined their ranks. He fell in at the rear and went by with the others."

Both play and novel end happily, although Tony and Janet marry without their parents' blessing or even knowledge, while, in the play, married bliss with Miranda is preceded by Ferdinand's restoration to his father. After the fight with Morelli, Maradick jettisons his adulterous feeling for Mrs. Lester and returns with his wife to the college town of Epsom—paralleling Prospero's return to a secluded life in Naples. Walpole, an avid Shakespeare reader, was not of course trying to "novelize" or modernize *The Tempest;* he simply adapted some of its aspects. (To interested readers I leave the pleasure of identifying others besides those mentioned here.) Despite this tour de force, *Maradick at Forty*, for the reasons noted earlier, does not quite succeed as a novel. Another flaw is its verboseness. As Clemence Dane comments (166), the "characters say every single thing that they have ever thought or felt, aloud and twice over." Nature descriptions, dripping with personification, and satirical passages share alike an arch prolixity of detail. If an outpouring of heedless energy, fancy, and inventiveness alone could make a book succeed, *Maradick at Forty* would have established Walpole's permanent reputation. That happy event awaited his third novel instead.

IV Mr. Perrin and Mr. Traill

Commercially speaking, *Mr. Perrin and Mr. Traill* (1911) is Walpole's most long-lived novel. Critically speaking, until re-

HUGH WALPOLE

cently, it has been one of his best regarded works. Its quick
commercial success stemmed partly, at first, from its being a
roman à clef. "About 1910 H. G. Wells gave his famous lecture
at the Times' Book Club," Walpole later recalled, "in which he
declared, that we had had enough of romantic nonsense and that
novels must deal with real people and be afraid of nothing." [12]
This invitation, coming from one of his special mentors, was seized
on by the young author, who emerged in two months with *Perrin
and Traill*. Despite the Cornish setting, it was obviously a tran-
scription of the year he had spent at Epsom College teaching
French—except that he neither committed suicide like Vincent
Perrin, nor like Archie Traill, caused anyone else to do so. (The
American version, *The Gods and Mr. Perrin*, has a different ending; see the discussion below.)

As a study of madness, *Perrin* is obvious enough not to puzzle
its audience and sympathetic enough not to alienate them. After
the novel's initial *succès de scandale*, based on the recognizabil-
ity of both its characters and setting, its popularity with the public
probably derived from the exotic idea of a pundit schoolmaster
choosing to die (in the English version, not in the American one)
so that a happy-go-lucky young colleague might live. But its long-
time reputation among critics—often to the detriment of Walpole's later work—is, frankly, harder to understand. Three years
after it was published, Arnold Bennett asserted:

I say it is a solemn thing to discover an authentic novelist. In the
author of *Mr. Perrin and Mr. Traill* I discovered one. The hand of the
born and consecrated novelist is apparent in *Mr. Perrin and Mr. Traill*.
You cannot read it, and then say it isn't true. You cannot read it and
then say it isn't beautiful. You may if you choose assert that there
is a strain of psychological morbidity in Mr. Walpole's powerful gift.
I shall not contradict you. I shall merely say that I like it. . . . Whatever Mr. Walpole may or may not do in the future; . . . 'Mr. Perrin
and Mr. Traill' will stand. [13]

As a prophecy, the last sentence proved only too true, to the
despair of Perrin's creator, who asserted that even *Jeremy at
Crale*, his minor novel about schoolboys, was better than his
famous novel about schoolmasters. "But will critics say so? Never
on their life." [14] A main reason for the kind reception may have
been its brevity in a time when most novels ran much longer, for

[34]

favorable analysts saw *Perrin and Traill* as a vignette making its point exquisitely and poignantly within a small compass. And the point made was new: the problems of the English schoolboy were a familiar subject in English fiction, but those of the English schoolmaster were not. Amazing as it seems today, *Mr. Perrin and Mr. Traill* was the first fictional treatment of English public-school life from the teacher's viewpoint since Dickens' *Nicholas Nickleby*. Walpole minced no words in describing the strained conditions in a typical public school, not only between teacher and pupil (the traditional angle) but also, and more importantly, between teacher and teacher and teacher and headmaster.

Finally, the critics admired its reality. Of course, as a roman à clef, it employed real people, events, and setting. But by "realism" they meant that it illustrated certain traits attributed by consensus to the Realistic novel: "natural" diction, an emphasis on life's tediums as experienced by the common man or woman in believable circumstances, and a reluctance on the writer's part to provide a happy ending. That Vincent Perrin is an antihero, sadly flawed, vulnerable, even physically unattractive, also assures the novel's "realism." "You cannot read it, and then say it isn't true," Bennett had written. "You cannot read it and then say it isn't beautiful." Presumably this last adjective refers to the final scene where Perrin, with a Sidney Carton-like gesture of "It is a far, far better thing that I do than I have ever done," throws away his life in order to save the life of the youth he has viewed as his worst enemy. The reader, if he takes this kind of quasi-tragedy seriously, as the English critics and public apparently did, may find it elevating.

Walpole's American publishers, however, disliked the ending: they thought it too serious, too "morbid" for the tenderhearted American public. My own reasons for preferring the ending of the American edition, *The Gods and Mr. Perrin*, are the same as Walpole's, who wrote in his diary when making the change: "It will be *such* an improvement . . . much more logical and convincing—wish I had done it originally" (April 16, 17, 1911). In both versions, the first eighty percent is the same. The novel marks a change from the basically ebullient mood of *Maradick*'s tour de force. *Perrin* too contains satire, but its grim jibes are woven directly into the plot. Every petty detail of school life presented to the reader through the satirical eye of the deuteragonist, Traill, and, especially in the American version, of Perrin himself, is a stone in the wall of that living crypt, Moffatt's Academy, which stands on a hill overlooking the sea near Pendragon, Cornwall (Archie Traill knows Robin Trojan).

The hill represents the lamentable distance between the school —by extension, any school—and "real life." "How little people realized!" reflects attractive Isabel Desart, a friend of one of the faculty wives: "all those crowded, stifled souls buried of their own original free-will beneath fantastic piles of scribbled paper, cursing their fate, but unable to escape from it." "The holidays come, and you go out into the world to find that you are different from all other men," one of the older teachers tells Traill. The hill also suggests poor Vincent Perrin's Sisyphus-like struggles as he tries to surmount a regrettable personality. A kind of English Ichabod Crane, Perrin, we learn, was unpopular even as a boy; now, in his late thirties, he is a nervous, petty tyrant.

When Archie Traill, a young four-square, former football star, comes to teach at Moffatt's, he is immediately popular with the other masters and with the students, including Perrin's favorite pupil. Before long, Traill makes Perrin look ridiculous in what their amused colleagues dub the "Battle of the Umbrella"; worst of all, he gains the love of Isabel Desart, whom Mr. Perrin dreams of marrying. Whereupon Perrin, affected by the growing tensions of the term, "that evil spirit that they all . . . seemed to feel as the weeks gathered in numbers," loses his head and decides to murder Mr. Traill, then commit suicide. Meanwhile, sensitive to the dry rot permeating Moffatt's from the headmaster down, Traill agrees with Isabel that he is unsuited to academic life, and resigns, effective at the end of the term.

On the last day, Prize Day exercises are held—and here the English and American versions part company. In the original, Mr. Perrin, miserable and silent, sits through the hypocritical twaddle handed parents and students by the headmaster and the Board; then he goes to his room and waits. Snoozing fitfully, about dawn he hears Traill leave his room, which is across the hall. Grabbing a knife, Perrin follows him outdoors and down to the cliff overlooking the sea. After a tirade recounting his grievances, he lunges forward, knife in hand—whereat Traill recoils, trips, and plunges to the sand below. He lies motionless; the tide is rising; and Mr. Perrin, shocked into sanity, half-falls, half-scrambles down to his "enemy," whom he finds unconscious but still alive. Cradling Traill in his bony arms, he lifts him onto a narrow ledge above the reach of the tide; then, exulting in his conviction that by saving the young man's life he has made his own worthwhile, he leaps forward to the sea and death. In the next section (still in the English version), Isabel is told of Traill's accident and of Perrin's sacrifice. A few pious words are spoken; and, on the last page, Perrin's former star pupil, ignorant of what has happened, decides to be nicer to his old teacher "next term." Both scenes, combining domestic Realism with melodrama and introducing a touch of irony, seem designed to cushion the suicide.

The Gods and Mr. Perrin may not be more in line with today's tastes, for "tastes" change rapidly and right now in America melodrama has a genuine appeal; but certainly the American version is less contrived, more convincing, than the English. At the Prize Day exercises, Perrin, repelled by the anodynes handed down from the platform, leaps to his feet to deliver a brief but stirring diatribe against the school. "It is all hell here . . . hell!" he concludes, and rushes back to his room revenged, not on Traill, whom he now forgives, but on the system, Moffatt's itself, the cause in the first place of his murderous impulse. He swaggers a little, for surely his equally harassed fellows will thank him for his outburst.

But he has another lesson in humility to learn. Instead of praise from his colleagues and outrage from the administration, he meets respectively with furtive avoidance and sympathy; his speech is considered an aberration, a sign that he needs rest. Ironically, young Traill half-understands and, in the only terms he knows, expresses approval:

". . . I wanted to tell you—that—well—oh, that I thought you were awfully plucky this afternoon."

"Oh! Thank you. It wasn't plucky really—it was a very foolish thing to do."

"No—really—the other fellows didn't understand—"

"Oh, yes! They understood very well."

"But what did the boy know," Walpole adds, "what could the boy know, of the man's utter despair as he sat there through the night?" Heartsick, Perrin leaves his room the next morning, vaguely considering suicide (presumably in deference to the thin-skinned American public, Walpole is cagey here). On the path to the cliff he meets Isabel Desart, and his recapitulative harangue to Archie Traill in the English version is replaced by a dialogue in which she pleads with him to look on the harrowing semester just past as his training for a glorious future at Moffatt's.

"Think of the pluck of it—after all that has happened—to come back, knowing what they think of you, knowing what you think of yourself. . . . I believe the only thing we're in the world for is to have courage—that answers everything—and some of us have such fat, easy lives that we've no chance at all. But you to come back with your teeth set, to build it all up again, to will it all back! Oh! It's splendid! And Archie and I will have our happy, ordinary existences—just going along—and you'll be here doing the finest thing in the world."

Obviously, neither ending is free from sentimentality; but the American one, with its emphasis on "positive confrontation," seems at least as suitable, if not more so, for present-day audiences than does the melodramatic English close with its overtones of pious self-sacrifice. In both versions, the theme is psychological as well as social. Vincent Perrin becomes indisputably mad, in both, and his lunacy is caused by the school. The main danger is that, by splitting the reader's emotions between compassion for Perrin and amused horror at the procedures which produce Perrins, the author may blur his effects. The subplot, involving Mrs. Comber, Isabel's faculty-wife friend, and her marital troubles, is another distraction.

A special edition of the novel published by Everyman's Library in 1935 was reissued in 1955. At that time, Cyril Connolly, one of the critics who had insisted that *Perrin and Traill* was Walpole's masterpiece, finally saw it in perspective. Walpole was right in protesting that *Perrin* was not that good, said Mr. Connolly: "What were we thinking about? Yet 'Mr. Perrin and Mr. Traill' is perfectly readable, even mildly enjoyable . . . [and it] ends in a cosy tragedy." [15] *Mr. Perrin and Mr. Traill*, with its "cosy tragedy," continues to be published in England. Its enlightened counterpart, *The Gods and Mr. Perrin*, should be revived, at least in paperback, by some American publisher.

V *A Pattern: The Pursued Protagonist*

Mr. Perrin and Mr. Traill was the first Walpole plot to be built openly around a pattern that dominates his fiction more than most readers realize: the pattern of the pursued protagonist. The surname "Traill" indicates the young man's image in the mind of Vincent Perrin, who feels that Traill is following him. He comes to teach at the school where Perrin teaches, preempts the bathtub when Perrin wants it, absconds with Perrin's umbrella on a stormy day, lures Perrin's star pupil away, and, worst of all, attracts the same young woman Perrin wants to marry. Vincent Perrin's reactions to all this are ambivalent. His ego-response is paranoid—he develops what is aptly called a "persecution complex" against Traill. At the same time, he is drawn to Traill, subconsciously, as his "double," his *doppelgänger*, insofar as the young man complements Perrin's own nature. Physically and temperamentally his opposite—sturdy where he is thin; placid where he is nervous—Traill represents Perrin as he would like to be.

Walpole does not emphasize this point in the novel, thus the reader is apt to pass it by. Henry James, complaining about Traill, wrote to his friend: "I don't quite understand why . . . you . . . take such pains to demonstrate that Mr. Traill was, as a vessel of experience, absolutely *nil*." [16] James failed to see that Traill exists chiefly in Perrin's apprehension of him as a part of his own personality, and needs, therefore, no more depth than an image in a mirror. The novel's structure is to blame: by dividing the narrative viewpoint among Perrin, Traill, Isabel, and Isabel's friend Mrs. Comber, Walpole creates far too many centers of consciousness. Had he stayed with Perrin's, the doubles pattern in all its ramifications would have been clearer.

Counterpoised to Traill in the splitting that takes place in Perrin's mind is the "grey figure," a desiccated pessimist with an instinct for failure: his own worst traits sorted out and re-imaged as a shadow whom he calls "the other Mr. Perrin." "There were always three of them now—himself, the other Mr. Perrin, and Traill—they always went about together," he reflects at one point. In the American version, after Perrin's Prize Day outburst, both figures—the hallucinated "Traill" and "the other Mr. Perrin"—leave; but, when Perrin realizes that only Traill (the real Traill) has appreciated his bravery, the "grey figure" returns to urge

Perrin to kill himself. In the American version, of course, he does not do so. In the English version—for whatever altruistic reasons —he does, saving Traill's life in the process.

In four of Walpole's later novels where the pursued-protagonist pattern is used—*Above the Dark Circus, The Fortress, The Inquisitor*, and *The Killer and the Slain*—both pursued and pursuer are destroyed, justifiably (morally speaking) in every case except that of the pursued in *The Fortress*. Several stories follow the *Perrin* pattern: death of the pursued only. In *The Old Ladies*, on the other hand, the guiltless victim dies while the vicious pursuer lives, thereby adding to the horror of the story. In the holocausts of *Above the Dark Circus* and of *The Inquisitor*, two brothers figure as pursuer and pursued. This pattern in lighter vein recalls Shakespeare's *Comedy of Errors*, where two sets of identical twins, each unknown to his brother, sow confusion among the citizens of Ephesus. Walpole's repertoire doesn't include identical twins, but he sometimes uses the pursued-protagonist pattern for comedy as in *The Young Enchanted, Farthing Hall* (co-author J. B. Priestley), and *The Joyful Delaneys*. Most examples, however, are neither tragic (resulting in death) nor comic (pure spoof). Typical is *Maradick at Forty*, where the shadowing creates a problem but where the outcome is not fatal. Maradick and Tony Gale often feel that Morelli is following them. Sometimes he actually is; at other times they imagine it, as Perrin does about Traill. But they do not become paranoid, and the only creature that dies is a small dog.

Perrin, as we saw, is a more serious case. The first half of the story—Traill's arrival at the school, the umbrella and bathtub incidents, his annexing of Perrin's star pupil and finally of Isabel— illustrates "pursuit" in a metaphorical sense only: a secondary character, younger in this case (sometimes the gap is economic), enters into and follows the protagonist's "life style." This pattern is found, less overtly, in *Maradick at Forty*: Tony Gale "follows" Maradick to the same resort hotel; later they dance arm in arm around the town; they fall in love on the same day but, fortunately, not with the same person; and their romances are resolved on the same day, each in an appropriate manner.

To summarize, the pursued-protagonist pattern as I have described it has three forms—(a) the protagonist is physically shadowed; (b) the protagonist *feels* that he is being physically

shadowed by a person or persons actually not there; (c) the protagonist is shadowed metaphorically by someone who adopts a
career or a life style similar to the protagonist's. Any or all of these
can occur in a single novel, as in *Maradick* we find all of them;
in *Perrin*, only two. These patterns represent a radical simplifica-
tion of those described in Robert Rogers' excellent study *The
Double in Literature*.[17] "Double" is certainly the right term for
what occurs in "b" and "c," but I find it harder to apply it to "a"—
which Mr. Rogers himself does as an afterthought.[18] On the other
hand, my cover-all phrase "pursued protagonist" is cumbersome
and sometimes inaccurate: the deuteragonist, for example, may
be the one pursued. In any case, the reader can doubtless pick
out elements of the pattern himself as he reads the following
chapters. The related term "inversion" has special meaning for
novels like *The Wooden Horse*, where the deuteragonist, moving
in an opposite direction from the protagonist, acts as his opposing
or inverted double. Thus, Robin ends his love affair as Harry
starts his; Harry becomes more conventional as Robin becomes
less so, and so on. Inverted doubles also occur in several other
novels. Doubling for contrast and doubling for intensification
seem to have intrigued Walpole equally.

CHAPTER 3

Artist

STILL tingling from the excitement of writing fictionalized autobiography in *Mr. Perrin and Mr. Traill,* Walpole embarked next on a *Künstlerroman,* that is, the story of an artist—in this case a young writer whose experience in some ways again resembled Walpole's. Based on the unpublished "Troy Hanneton," the novel was called *Fortitude.* Then a hitch occurred, as Hart-Davis explains: "[Hugh's] contract compelled him to give his next book to Mills & Boon [publishers of *Perrin*], but *Fortitude* had all along been designed to be his *magnum opus* and for it he would prefer a younger, more fashionable firm. He had his eye on Martin Secker. . . . After much deliberation it was decided that Hugh should lay aside *Fortitude* and dash off a shorter novel for Mills & Boon" (85). The result was *Prelude to Adventure,* a minor work with a religious theme which will be discussed below in Chapter 5.

Hitherto this study of Walpole has been presented chronologically; but, from the present chapter on, the works are considered thematically in order to bring out more clearly the diverse aspects of Walpole's creative career. Each theme centers around a work recognized as outstanding at the time, and these are considered in order: *Fortitude* (1913), *The Dark Forest* (1916), *The Cathedral* (1922), *Wintersmoon* (1928), and *Rogue Herries* (1930). Around them are grouped other titles whose content is relevant to the theme. *Fortitude,* for example, is one of three novels spaced throughout Walpole's career dealing with artist-heroes; the others are *Hans Frost* (1929) and *John Cornelius* (1937). A discussion of these novels, with their common theme, is the concern of this present chapter.

I   Fortitude

The first and last parts of *Fortitude* take place in Treliss, Cornwall, the setting of *Maradick at Forty.* Gothic though the backgrounds are—Scaw House, where Peter Westcott lives; the old inn where the story opens; the antique shop of Peter's friend Zachary Tan—they are treated more matter-of-factly than similar settings in *Maradick*. The spectres that crowd Peter's mind are those of Ibsen's play *Ghosts;* for, as he grows up, Peter is worried more and more about his heredity. He fears that his father and grandfather, a loathsome pair, have passed their weaknesses on to him and that sooner or later he must succumb. Peter, driven by his fear, becomes a traditional figure—the Sensitive Young Man from the Provinces who leaves his unhappy home to seek a fortune midst the alluring uncertainties of the metropolis.

In London, Peter lives first in a Bloomsbury boardinghouse. He works at a bookshop near Trafalgar Square and becomes the unwitting companion of anarchists who are plotting against Queen Victoria. The plot fails, the shop closes, and he moves to Cheapside, where he nearly starves while waiting for his first novel to be published. When it is, it enjoys immediate success. He marries the charming but irresponsible Clare and buys her a house in Chelsea—only to see both career and marriage disintegrate after his infant son dies. His sense of fatalism draws him back to Treliss, where his repellent old grandfather had warned him before he left, "Mind you, boy, . . . if you don't get the better of the Devil you'll be just like me one of these days. So he'll [Peter's father] be, my son, one day. Just like me—and then it'll be your turn, my boy. Oh, they Westcotts! . . . I was strong once, boy, hegh, hegh! Indeed I was, just like your father—and he'll be just like me, one day! Oh! yes, he will—blast his bones! . . . We all come to it."

Haunted by this warning and sure that he will never "get the better of the Devil," Peter returns prepared to surrender to the family curse, join his father's debauches (the grandfather is now dead), and drink himself into an early grave. He is not allowed to do so; for Norah Monogue, a selfless London friend who is ill and who has come to Treliss to die, assures him that moral strength has more power than heredity. Peter promises to prove his self-mastery by returning to London; and, before he leaves he climbs a hill and, during a thunderstorm, hears "Voices" proclaiming a credo of self-reliance:

Blessed be all Loss and the Failure of Friends and the Sacrifice of love. . . .

Blessed be the Destruction of all Possessions, the Ruin of all Property, Fine Cities, and Great Palaces. . . .

Blessed be the Disappointment of all Ambitions. . . .

Blessed be these Things—for of these things cometh the making of a man. . . .

Peter "answer[s] the storm: . . . 'Make me brave! Make me brave!'" Interesting though these sentiments may be, the supernatural scene, coming at the end of an otherwise Realistic novel, surprises the reader; and post-adolescents today may find its bombast irritating.

At the time it was published, *Fortitude* was an even bigger success than *Mr. Perrin and Mr. Traill:* "promise was beginning to pass into achievement," Rupert Hart-Davis observes (197); "and with this, his fifth novel, Hugh was promoted to that interminable formation, the 'front rank of contemporary novelists.'" It is poetically fitting that his first novel about a novelist brought about this recognition. From being an acolyte at the altar of literature, he was now one of the writer-priests themselves. The theme of *Fortitude,* stated quaintly in the first two sentences by an ancient seaman, is "'Tisn't life that matters. 'Tis the courage you bring to it"; and this became a trumpet call on the lips of clergymen and teachers.

The few demurrals about the novel were from individuals like Arnold Bennett, who preferred the first half, and Henry James, who preferred the second. A respected literary journal claimed the novel to be one of the four "finds" of 1913 that included D. H. Lawrence's *Sons and Lovers;* and fourteen years later the Pratt Institute Free Library of Brooklyn, New York, included it in a list of "fifty titles selected from the best fiction in all tongues, produced in the first quarter of this century." [1]

I would hesitate to cavil about a work so well regarded were my doubts not shared by the author, who labelled it "a hotchpotch" (Diary, May 31, 1919). To be represented in Modern Library had been one of Walpole's "early ambitions" (Diary, Feb. 13, 1930), but he was amazed in 1930 when its publishers asked for *Fortitude.* The reasons he finally fixed on,[2] its vigor and sincerity, are the most valid ones.

The story is absorbing enough; and, except for attempts at dialect, the diction is well enough managed; but the constant sobriety is boring, and the unities in so long a work are hard for the reader to keep in mind. An abridged version was issued in 1938, edited apparently by Walpole himself, where the loss of discursive ramblings and supererogative vignettes constitutes a real gain. I should be glad to support *Fortitude* in the abridged form as a classic, although unfortunately it is out of print and hard to find.

II Hans Frost

In *Fortitude*, Peter Westcott's career as a writer is viewed from two standpoints: the commercial, his relative earnings or lack thereof and how long it takes him to write; and the social, the reaction of his family and friends to his career as a writer, and his relationships with other writers, friendly or not. Overall, there hangs an air of excitement about the creative process itself; and, in this respect, Peter's attitude coincides with his author's. But for more solid clues about Walpole's career we must turn to *Hans Frost* (1929) and to *John Cornelius* (1937).

Despite its use of a writer-hero, *Hans Frost* in many ways is the antithesis of *Fortitude*. Hans is seventy; Peter Westcott, at the end, twenty-nine. *Hans Frost* covers a single month, *Fortitude,* seventeen years. Clare, Peter's selfish young wife, leaves him for another after a marriage of two years; but Hans, after twenty years, leaves his selfish, middle-aged wife in order to write the masterpiece she has kept him from writing. That the personalities of the two men differ can be seen without recourse to *Fortitude* itself since Peter is also a character in *Hans Frost*. A younger fellow writer of Hans's, he is still earnest and idealistic. Hans, on the contrary, is impatient with life and alternately deals out cynicism and kindness, as people and events move him to do. We learn more of Hans the Author than we ever do of Peter in the same capacity. Some aspects, to be sure, are social: his fellow authors' presentation to Hans of a Manet on his seventieth birthday; vignettes (à clef) of specific authors and critics; an amusing description of a literary dinner; and the general hubbub involved in being a prominent author, especially one cursed with a managing wife.

In place of the vague excitement that Peter—and the reader—feel in *Fortitude* whenever the subject of writing comes up, a specific excitement rises in *Hans Frost* directly from Hans's dilemma as he waits, almost praying, for inspiration for his novel: "a voice that will cry, 'Now—BEGIN!'" He hopes the voice will come; but, until he decides to go to Cornwall, he is not at all sure that it will. His attitude toward the writing he did in the past is sardonic but tinged with nostalgia. Readers oriented toward bibliography will be fascinated by Chapter IV, "A la Recherche du Temps Perdu," in which Hans runs his eye along the spines of a shelf of his books. Like Walpole himself, Frost is a man of letters. He has written mostly novels, also essays, a book of travels, and poetry: twenty-three volumes in all; and Walpole supplies a date and title for each.

In Chapter I, Nathalie Swan, Mrs. Frost's niece, while on her way to London by train, mentally mulls over the books by Hans that she has liked (she has never met him). His fellow writers present the Manet in Chapter III, and the literary dinner takes place in Chapter IV. Thus the reader is strongly aware, through the first half of the book, of Frost's position as a writer. For a while the story becomes Nathalie's; then, after she flees from London, we see Hans trying once more to write his masterpiece, but failing, in the gilded cage that he has permitted his wife to build around him.

The last scene in Cornwall is effective. He is watching a great wave break on the shore:

At that moment, in Hans' ears, a voice cried: "now—BEGIN!"

He turned, crossed again the stone steps, mounted the steps to the cottage, climbed the dark stairs.

He entered the little white room, closed the door behind him, sat down at the deal table, drew the pad of papers before him, wrote:

THE ONE-EYED COMMANDER

I

Then his pen moved swiftly.

The voice at the end of *Hans Frost* tells the protagonist to write; those at the end of *Fortitude* tell Peter to be a brave man. Hans, following his creative behest, seems younger than Peter. Certainly the book as a whole is fresher and more spontaneous than *Fortitude*. Walpole wrote in his diary (June 7, 1927), "I like this book. It's in a new vein for me, the vein of humour I ought to have tried long ago." Wit is scattered piecemeal through most of his books, in some more than in others; but *Hans Frost* is

unique for its outpouring of epigrams, wry sallies, and airy
monologues. Impossible to quote out of context, they nevertheless
divert the reader.

Underneath the story line is a pattern we met in *Maradick:*
an older man profits from a young girl's flight to freedom. Maradick, having aided Tony to free Janet Morelli from her father's
influence, is himself inspired to shake off the influence of Mrs.
Lester. Like Janet, Nathalie Swan in *Hans Frost* is only nineteen,
but twenty years of increased independence for women separate
the two novels. When Mrs. Frost tells Nathalie that Hans wants
her to go away and leave them alone (a lie), the girl goes to Cornwall to get a job. Struck by her courage, Hans deserts his shrew-
ish wife and follows Nathalie, not to be with her—his love for her
is not that kind—but to write, if possible, his masterpiece. After
working a while, Nathalie returns to London and marries an
ambitious young Russian émigré.

Although the novel begins with Nathalie and although she has
a full-scale "story" of her own, as a character she is not wholly
realized. In a novel whose main theme is "To write successfully,
a writer must be free," her role is that of Hans's liberator. As
Marguerite Steen has indicated, theirs is "a meeting of two sensi-
tives" (210). At the same time, Hans is by no means senile. His
feeling for his niece is not lascivious, but he is thoroughly aware
of her physically—and, healthily, she of him. Walpole later received this tribute from one of his male readers: [3]

I am 20 years your senior—I was born in 1864 so I am not far off
Hans Frost's age. . . . It is the first time I have ever read such an
absolutely truthful description of the psychology of an elderly man to
a young girl. It is *right—right* in every line you write. I know it from
experience—I have felt it all myself—but you are the first I have ever
known describe it—and because it is so true—it will live. Nor am I
ashamed to confess that you have made plain to me what was nebulous
and confused in my own mind.

That's all I want to say. You cannot resent honest appreciation can
you?

Reviews were especially good. None regarded Hans as an
escapist or felt that he should have stayed in London and subdued
his still beautiful wife. To suggest it would have been to take
the book more seriously than it deserved or than Walpole in-

tended. It would have been a "problem novel" like *Fortitude* or *John Cornelius,* his next story with a writer-protagonist. Of the three, my own preference is for *Hans Frost;* for I feel as Virginia Woolf did when she wrote about it to Walpole: "We had visitors and I had an article to write and books to read, and there I sat reading on and on and on, pretending that I would only read one more chapter and then stop; and then arguing that as there were only five more chapters I might as well finish. . . . There's a general radiancy and Christmas tree lustre that I find adorable." [4] As a way of mentally "bridging the generation gap," I recommend it also to younger readers.

III   John Cornelius

In August, 1935, while en route to Hollywood, where Walpole was slated to write scripts for *Little Lord Fauntleroy* and "Kim," he started his third novel about a writer, *John Cornelius* (1937). "I look forward to this book hugely, for I feel that I may be free and personal and spontaneous in it, and Cornelius himself is already as real to me as myself," says his diary (Aug. 2, 1935). Cornelius, in fact, *became* Hugh Walpole as he continued writing, more than Hans Frost or Peter Westcott had ever been. John's childhood and his appearance owe something to Hans Christian Andersen's,[5] whose first name the author had already borrowed for Hans Frost, showing how closely Walpole identified that superb writer of children's stories with the trials of professional authorship. But, as John grows older, his life and especially his philosophy became increasingly like his creator's, who wrote to Harold Macmillan on August 27, 1937 that "I shall never . . . expose as much of myself in a novel again!"

This merging of himself with his protagonist resulted, unfortunately, in a story steeped in nostalgic pathos and much longer than its plot demands. I am tempted to call it a "problem novel"; for John has problems: like Peter Westcott, of attending an unpleasant school; like Peter and Hans Frost, of choosing a shallow wife; and of gaining fame from the fairy tales he tosses off and despises, instead of from the serious fiction on which he spends so much time and thought. The term "problem novel," however, supposes a Realistic approach that is absent from *John Cornelius.* True, the outer trappings are there. The story is presented as biography: a potpourri of the memories of the first-person narrator, who knew John personally, as well as of diary excerpts, letters, and interviews. But the atmosphere is of a particularly fatuous kind as the biographer, the interviewees, and John himself (through his diary) collaborate to produce what seems like a series of fairy tales with John Cornelius as the hero. Fantastic old women, crazy old men, the sea, clouds, colors, animals, bosom friends, fearful enemies, and mystic visions are stuffed into a four-hundred-page packet apparently meant to be taken seriously.

There is too much telling, not enough showing. First we are told of John's ancestors, then of his luckless father, his artless mother, and finally of small John himself in their poor Glebeshire home surrounded by weird neighbors, including a female trio he calls "The Three Witches." The father's luck goes from bad to worse; eventually, he dies; and John leaves home to seek the fortune his proud mother expects him to find. Completely uneducated herself, she stands in awe of her talented son. The rest of the book draws on Walpole's own experiences as a schoolteacher and (in pages studded with thinly disguised portraits) as a member of London literary circles. A mystical vision experienced by John during World War I in France is similar to one that Walpole had in Russia.

Returned home and unhappily married, John's growing frustration at being praised for the writings he thinks least of and criticized for the ones he values most is again like Walpole's (and most authors' perhaps). When his best friend, Charlie Christian, dies, Cornelius loses the will to live. His death at thirty-seven, of a heart attack, in the arms of his foremost "enemy" among the London literary critics after their reconciliation, is one that Walpole may have envisioned for himself. Because Walpole took their remarks personally, his relations with critics were apt to be strained. He fought his weakness and penned frequent fervent apologies; but, when matters went too far, a "deathbed" reconciliation like John's probably seemed the only solution.

Too lethargic for fantasy, too bland for romance, this novel is hard to categorize. It is not comedy, not tragedy. If Cornelius has a tragic flaw, it is his excruciating sensitivity, making it hard for him, after the age of six, to enjoy life very much. Cornelius' biographer refuses to consider his death a tragedy: "I myself feel that he had given the world, in his fairy-stories, the work that he was intended to do. . . . In his personal life he was, I am sure, a restless stranger on this earth." The wording of this pronouncement, the hero's initials, J. C., and his best friend's name, Charlie Christian, make it plain that we are dealing with hagiography. In aura, technique, and content *John Cornelius* is a modern version of a Medieval genre, the saint's life. To his sister, Walpole complained that the reviews were "completely non-understanding. Not one . . . paid any attention to the book's mystical side." [6] The *Church Times* especially disappointed him; for the anonymous reviewer wrote that, "If at times [Cornelius] has personality, it is that of a dreadful egotist and a confirmed bore." "Technique . . . cannot compensate for the lack of vision, of humour, of charm." [7] We do not look for those qualities in a saint's life, of course; but, on the other hand, readers could hardly be expected to sift through so much verbiage and discover, in one reading, the novel's religious theme. How many, for instance, would see that the following statements, sown helter-skelter through John's final letter to his "biographer," constitute a religious creed, a strange mixture of fatalism and Transcendentalism?

. . . I think from now on I'm going to be able to remove my unhappiness. . . . *But that isn't the point.* The point really is that I was always certain that there was a miraculous state of being just round the corner if I could only find it. . . . I was always sure that this wonderful *place* was about to appear. . . . They talk about "Above the Battle," but I think that [it] is really 'Below the Battle'—that just below all this noise and confusion and hatred the real life is continuous, always there waiting for us to find it. . . . Everyone is given their conditions within which they live—and *those* are the conditions they are given—none other. . . . I've always thought fidelity was the thing—fidelity to work, to people, to ideals. But only now at last I understand the greater fidelity—to life itself which is, I believe, given to me to use in such a shape—yes, in just this shape and no other. It may be that with death only I will find reality. . . .

In originality of technique, the novel is superior to *Fortitude* and *Hans Frost*. For reading pleasure, however, I would rank it about with *The Wooden Horse*, Walpole's first novel. Half of *Cornelius* was composed in Hollywood along with the script of *Little Lord Fauntleroy*, which is hagiography also. Today the film seems dated; *John Cornelius* only seems dull.

IV *The Question of Imitation*

Walpole clearly intended *Fortitude,* his best known story about a writer, to be the modern *David Copperfield.* Along with Fielding's *Tom Jones,* Smollett's *Peregrine Pickle,* and three books by "Henry Galleon" (Henry James), *David Copperfield* is one of the well-thumbed books on Peter's shelf. The man he most admires as a boy and who later saves him from starving in London is Stephen Brent, a Cornish fisherman turned farmer, who has the massive build of David's seaman friend, Ham Peggotty, in *Copperfield.* Peter's mother, like David's, is ill-treated by her husband and dies when the boy is young; and Peter's brutal whipping by his father is reminiscent of David's beating by his stepfather. Subsequently, David's bottle factory and Peter's prep school "become purgatories together." [8]

When Cardillac, a superior schoolfriend, appears on the scene, Peter calls him "my Steerforth." Later Clare, Peter's wife, runs away with the handsome, devil-may-care Cardillac as Little Em'ly Peggotty does with Steerforth. Clare is fragile, beautiful, and wealthy like David's wife Dora; and, if Peter only realized it, he has a "true love" in Norah Monogue as David Copperfield has in Agnes Wickfield.

But the parallels with *Copperfield,* while extensive and obvious, are not the only echoes in *Fortitude.* With some glee Walpole listed in his diary (Dec. 24, 1910 and Apr. 28, 1911) other works whose palpable influence, he felt, could be traced in his own novel: Thackeray's *Vanity Fair,* Emily Brontë's *Wuthering Heights,* Balzac's *Illusions Perdues,* Conrad's *Secret Agent,* Hall Caine's *Christian,* and some more obscure titles. To trace these influences in *Fortitude* would be a difficult but not impossible task. Yet, even if we were to attempt it, what of Walpole's other novels? Parallels between *Maradick at Forty* and Shakespeare's *The Tempest* were discussed in Chapter 2; but *Maradick* contains effects from other works too. Walpole's diary does not help us there— in fact, the list he provides for *Fortitude* is unique—but alert readers will detect signs of E. M. Forster's two Anglo-Italian novels, *Where Angels Fear to Tread* and *A Room with a View.*

Recalling that Walpole sent his first novel, *The Wooden Horse,* in manuscript to Forster and two other well-known writers, it is interesting to see some of the echoes that an Oxford reviewer found in it: "The background might have been taken direct from one of the Meredith novels— . . . and Mr. Galsworthy's books . . . have had their influence on Mr. Walpole. . . . Perhaps, however, the novelist one is most reminded of is Mr. Charles Marriott, in both 'The Column' and 'The House on the Sands.' " [9]

Marriott was one of the writers who read the manuscript. (Did he see the resemblances?) Both Forster and Galsworthy continued to influence Walpole; Forster's Cambridge novel, *The Longest Journey*, contributes to *Prelude to Adventure* (see below, Chapter 5); and Galsworthy's *Man of Property* does the same for *The Duchess of Wrexe* (see Chapter 6). Other elements in *The Duchess* can be traced to Henry James's *Golden Bowl* and to an essay on Madame du Deffand, a friend of Walpole's famous ancestor Horace, written by Lytton Strachey. *Hans Frost* owes something to Edith Wharton's *Ethan Frome*, and also something to Shakespeare's *Love's Labour's Lost*.

Among Walpole's early works, *Perrin and Traill* seems the least imitative; yet it is a roman à clef, as are some of his other novels. But what author can truthfully say that he never draws his characters from life? In any case, my study of Walpole is not an identification file; nor do I intend after this chapter to refer to the mixture of sources he undoubtedly drew upon when writing his novels. The lists of titles at the backs of his diaries show that he read, on the average, fifteen books a month. Some authors he read again and again, particularly Shakespeare and Marcel Proust; otherwise, he divided his time equally between new books and the classics, both fiction and nonfiction. Every month he attended at least a dozen plays and operas, additional stimuli to the creative process.

The young Walpole, who had started writing historical fiction at the age of thirteen by imitating his favorite authors, never quite lost the habit; but few critics down the years have mentioned this fact, aside from vague references to Dickens and Henry James. On the contrary, Walpole has often been considered a pace setter; and one of the first to so consider him was the American critic Joseph Warren Beach. "Mr. Walpole is of course a writer of great power and charm. He can handle plots, create atmosphere, invent characters and make them live as few novelists can do on either side of the Atlantic. He abounds in interesting stuff," Mr. Beach wrote. "He must have an enormous influence

over writers less original and less critical, and I am inclined to
hold him partly responsible for many false strokes in the work of
writers like Mr. Hutchinson." [10] (A. S. M. Hutchinson's novel *If
Winter Comes* was a best-seller at the time.) In 1952 the *Times
Literary Supplement* suggested that Virginia Woolf's *The Years*
was an imitation of Walpole's *Wintersmoon*.[11] Her *Between the
Acts* can be seen as a reworking of *The Inquisitor*, which may
also have influenced T. S. Eliot's *Murder in the Cathedral*—or
vice versa.[12]

What can be deduced from all this trading back and forth?
Possibly that art has as much right to imitate art as to imitate
the chimera called "life." What matters is what the artist does
with his material. Walpole made *Fortitude* "repetitive" (imitative), as he later explained, because "I knew . . . that . . . I would,
in the end, have imaginatively a larger scope for my creative
faculty than by the photographic representation of things that I
had myself seen but never imagined." [13] If tempted to smile at
this ingenious rationale, we recall that Shakespeare might have
said the same thing. In our own age (and Walpole's), T. S. Eliot
has made imitation seem the only possible way to write. Bewail-
ing "our tendency to insist, when we praise a poet, upon those
aspects of his work in which he least resembles any one else,"
Eliot adds:

We dwell with satisfaction upon the poet's difference from his predecessors, especially his immediate predecessors; we endeavour to find
something that can be isolated in order to be enjoyed. Whereas if we
approach a poet without this prejudice we shall often find that not only
the best, but the most individual parts of his work may be those in
which the dead poets, his ancestors, assert their immortality most
vigorously. And I do not mean the impressionable period of adolescence, but the period of full maturity. . . . Some one said: "The dead
writers are remote from us because we *know* so much more than they
did." Precisely, and they are that which we know.[14]

Eliot, of course, was pleading on behalf of better writers than
Walpole—on behalf of himself, for example. That Eliot and Mrs.
Woolf perhaps took some ideas from Hugh Walpole does not
compromise their reputations. Walpole, after listing in his diary
some of the works he drew on for *Fortitude*, added tranquilly

"—but my own hotch-potch after all" (Apr. 28, 1911). Eliot, Shakespeare, Walpole, Woolf—each has a right to his "own hotch-potch," no matter what its source. Our sole basis for judgment is its quality.

CHAPTER 4

Witness

I The Dark Forest

WALPOLE'S first Russian novel, *The Dark Forest* (1916), is one of his best works; the second, *The Secret City* (1919), won the first James Tait Black Memorial Prize. Although *The Dark Forest* is the better of the two, both are worth reading. *The Dark Forest*, a love story, happens in East Galicia during the Great Retreat by the Russians in the face of the German offensive early in World War I; *The Secret City* is an atmosphere-shrouded tale of the March, 1917, "Provisional" Russian Revolution. Because these are Walpole's only novels with non-English settings, we need some biography here. Not surprisingly, his first introduction to Russia was a novel, *Kronstadt* by Max Pemberton, he read in the 1890's. At twenty-two, Walpole's attention was captured by Turgenev; at twenty-eight, he thrilled to the new Constance Garnett translation of Dostoevski's *Brothers Karamazov*.[1] Into his own novels he put as much of Russia as he dared from a distance: a tattered band of Russian anarchists in *Fortitude*, a deceased Russian mother in *The Duchess of Wrexe*, an Englishman who, after living in Russia, returns home in *The Green Mirror*.

Meanwhile, deciding for the sake of his art to broaden his horizons, Walpole himself arranged through his agent to go to Russia, writing articles as he went. Before he could leave, World War I began; but his poor eyesight kept him from enlisting, so he pushed ahead, arriving in Moscow on September 24. There he joined the "Sanitar," which he described to Henry James as "the part of the Red Cross that does the rough work at the front, carrying men out of the trenches, helping in the base hospitals in every sort of way, doing every kind of rough job. They are an absolutely official body and I shall be one of the few (half-dozen) Englishmen in the world wearing Russian uniform. . . . . I have, first, six weeks' training in first aid at the hospitals here, and then I go off to the very 'frontiest of the front.' " [2]

One result of his experience was *The Dark Forest,* composed under unlikely conditions when the "frontiest of the front" became the Great Retreat. Much of the novel was taken from a special diary, whose crisp diction and syntax are employed by the narrator, Ivan Durward, in civilian life a journalist. He and the protagonist, John Trenchard, both represent the author. Durward is the objective recorder, while through Trenchard, Walpole's guilelessness and "Mr. Pooter" (accident-prone) aspects are revealed. More purehearted than Walpole's famous antihero Perrin, Trenchard is also more ludicrous—as when he loses his pants during the Retreat! The incident is pitiful, but the reader cannot help smiling, for things like that do happen to the Don Quixotes, the "Lucky Jims," the divine fools.

Durward is thirty-one; Trenchard, slightly younger. Both English, they are going to the Russian front as stretcher bearers. While terribly self-conscious, Trenchard cannot hide his joy at being engaged to the young Russian nurse, Marie Ivanovna Krassovsky, although she seems nervous about the engagement. The two Englishmen; two nurses; a Russian orderly and his friend, a Russian doctor, arrive at "O——," and join the Otriad (field hospital) under Dr. Alexei Petrovitch Semyonov.

At fifty Semyonov has had "a string of mistresses"; a skillful surgeon and a personable, virile man, he falls in love with Marie, and she with him. Trenchard releases her, blaming himself for her infatuation: ". . . why could he not have held to her, dominated her, as a strong man would have done? . . . So, all his life it had been—so, all his life it would be." Durward also is attracted to Marie Ivanovna; and the neighboring "Forest of S——," normally symbolizing fear, hallucination, and death, takes on sexual meaning as he watches Marie and Semyonov leave the camp for the forest one afternoon: "That pursuit—the excitement of the penetration in the dark forest—the thrill of the chase—those things were for the strong men, the brave women—not for the halt and maimed" (Durward's "bad leg" is symbolic). But he feels more compassion for Marie than passion.

In *The Dark Forest* there are actually two triangles, each composed of two men and a woman. As Semyonov, in the first triangle, is older and more sophisticated than Trenchard, so in the other one, steadfast, serene Dr. Nikitin is sounder than his rival (both are middle-aged), the Russian orderly, Vassilievitch, whose surname betrays his foolish nature. These triangles result in a fantastic plot that undermines the novel's "reality" but is also its most striking feature. Two men contending for a lovely maiden accidentally encounter two erstwhile rivals for an older, extraordinarily fine woman, Mrs. Nikitin, who has died before the novel opens. While Nikitin and Vassilievitch realize the plight of Trenchard and Semyonov, the reverse is not true since Nikitin and Vassilievitch have never confessed their rivalry even to each other. Only Durward knows their story.

In each triangle, the woman dies: Mrs. Nikitin is already dead; Marie Ivanovna is killed during a battle in the forest. Coincidences mount as each man hopes (Semyonov skeptically) for reunion after death with the woman he loves before his rival can attain that state. Scorning suicide, they wait for the Enemy in the forest to resolve the situation. At last the weaker man of each pair is killed—by the same Austrian bomb; and, though their rivals live on, they seem better fitted to do so. To the question "How can mankind explain death?," no real answer is given. Of the main figures who die, the two men desire death; but, in the case of life-loving Marie Ivanovna, either predestination or "blind chance" may be the answer. By not specifying which it is, in effect Durward-Walpole reiterates the message, "Death is the ultimate mystery," developed through the forest metaphor.

Semyonov denies that the Forest of S—— is sinister; and Marie, before she dies, thinks it fascinating; but to most of the Otriad the forest is loathsome—dark, hot one day and freezing the next, evil-smelling (it is dotted with corpses), and vast. In an important passage Durward observes that not Germany, but Death is the enemy. The Otriad with its repeated expeditions, collectively and singly, into the Forest of S—— becomes a microcosm of mankind as it tries to understand Death: "Somewhere in the heart of the deep forest the enemy was hiding. We would defeat him? . . . He had some plot, some hidden surprise? . . . At the same instant, out upon the same hunt, seeking the same answer to their mystery, were millions of our fellows."

The strengths of *The Dark Forest* are its universal theme, varied characters, and engrossing plot. To me, its greatest flaw is Trenchard's diary, quoted from sporadically during the novel, extensively at the end. Its style, in contrast to Durward's forth-rightness, is appropriately maundering; but, realistically speaking, how many diaries sound like novels? Yet so many novelists use the journal device that my criticism, to be valid, must deal with specifics. On that basis, I find Trenchard's diary more believable and thus less annoying than those in some other Walpole novels.

The Dark Forest is not my favorite Walpole title, nor was it his. He described it (Journal, September 30, 1924, and September 19, 1936) as his "best work artistically" in contexts that define "artistic" as "balanced, objective." With this analysis I agree. The two novels I rank above it, *Rogue Herries* and *The Cathedral* (see Chapters 7 and 5), seem "artistic" in a more affective way because of their warm tone, a tone lacking in *The Dark Forest*.

II The Secret City

In October, 1915, Walpole left Russia, returning four months later as head of the British Information Bureau in Petrograd. Although the bureau, created "to counter the very effective German propaganda to which the Russians were ceaselessly subjected" (Hart-Davis, 148), proved a failure, Walpole's duties kept him there from February, 1916, to November, 1917. After nine months of uphill labor, a "long talk with the Ambassador . . . , he asking my advice about what he is to say to the Czar on Monday concerning anti-English opinion here," gave Walpole a chance to speak plainly: "Told him pro-German opinion here chiefly a matter of blood and money, neither of which things we can change" (Diary, November [4], 1916). After the March Revolution, the bureau's position worsened; for, as Hart-Davis explains, the new government "looked upon [it] as the agent of a reactionary imperialistic power, and Hugh became steadily more depressed" (162). Released at last, Walpole departed on November 8, 1917, the day after the Bolshevik coup d'état. Next April he finished *The Secret City* (1919), the only serious novel about the Russian March Revolution written by an Englishman (or an American, for that matter) who was there when it happened.[3] Unfortunately Walpole had let his diary lapse a few months before the Revolution, resuming it only when hostilities commenced; thus the first chapters in *Secret City*, which lead up to the Revolution, lack the immediacy of *The Dark Forest*.

Another problem, one that puts the work a bit out of focus,

is Walpole's transplanting the "real" protagonist and his family
from Moscow to Petrograd, the setting of the novel. In 1914, Walpole had roomed in Moscow with a family like the Markovitches
—"a nice woman, a melancholy man and three children," as he
told Henry James.[4] The woman, who taught Walpole Russian,
was "excellent"; but "The melancholy man has fits of awful temper
—every third morning. On Monday I am woken by hearing his
voice raised in a shrill trembling scream and it goes on and on.
All Monday and Tuesday husband and wife don't speak. Wednes-
day morning he cries at breakfast, and is forgiven. Thursday
morning it begins again. He's very polite to me because they've
no money and I mean a living to them. He offers me cigarettes
and chocolates which he keeps warm in his pockets. He's an inventor. . . ."

In England, Walpole could easily relocate his characters—that
is, relocate their real-life models; but Russia was too alien to him.
The result of such transporting in *The Secret City* is a loss of
sharpness, not only in the characters but in the pictures of Petrograd itself. The novel also labors under a set of bog-and-reptile
images straight from Gothic fiction, and they are so poorly in-
tegrated as to be unbelievable. Petrograd's marsh origins provide
a justification for the monster, which is introduced too often to
be mere background detail but not often enough to act as a
permeating metaphor.

The narrator-deuteragonist again is Durward, who has remained in Russia. Living on the outskirts of Petrograd, haunted
by memories of the dead Marie Ivanovna and her pathetic admirer,
John Trenchard, he becomes involved with the Markovitch family
after learning that Mrs. Markovitch's uncle is Dr. Alexei Semyonov. As the pivotal figure of the plot, Semyonov the sophisticated
antagonist is played up even more than in *The Dark Forest*. As
a character, however, he faces greater competition: febrile, bom-
bastic Nicolai Markovitch is a gaudier protagonist than Trenchard; and other important male characters, including Durward,
also diffuse the spotlight.

The inventor's plucky wife, Vera, is the major female figure.
Hers is not a happy life. Her husband goads her into frequent
quarrels (see Walpole's letter to James), and her attempts to keep
her sister in line end when the girl elopes with a Bolshevik. Vera
herself loves Jerry Lawrence, who is attached to the British Em-

bassy and is an old schoolmate of Durward; but their tenderness is restrained by circumstances. Ignorant of politics yet wanting to be a good wife, Vera sympathizes with her husband's bafflement and frustration after the March Revolution; but, when she compares him to the undaunted Lawrence (a maturer Archie Traill), her sympathy changes to scorn. Rejected, Markovitch becomes easy prey for the designs of Semyonov, who desires to drive his nephew-in-law to the point of murder.

The doctor's strange acts result from his loss of Marie. To Henry Bohun, the Markovitches' English boarder, Durward explains that, since her death, Semyonov has been "Really desolate, in a way that only your thorough sensualist can be. A beautiful fruit just within his grasp, something at last that can tempt his jaded appetite . . . it's gone, and gone, perhaps, into some one else's hands"—John Trenchard's. "There may be another life—who can really prove there isn't? . . . He's a man now ruled by an obsession." Suicide? "No, to a proud man like Semyonov that's a miserable confession of weakness. How they'd laugh at him, these other despicable human beings, if he did that!" Instead, he launches a program of vicious mental persecution against Markovitch—"first commending and then sneering at his inventions, playing upon his sensitiveness, [and] destroying his beliefs" (Steen, 128) in his wife and in his country.

The growing violence inside the family circle illustrates the violence outside it. On the historic date of May 1, 1917, Markovitch pursues his tormenter (the pursuer now pursued) to an empty palace in Katerinhof Park, which is noisy elsewhere with proletarian festivities. There he shoots Semyonov, as his victim has hoped and intended, then he shoots himself. Durward, who has followed them, runs to Markovitch: "Even as I held him, I heard coming closer and closer the rough triumphant notes of the 'Marseillaise.' "

The novel's theme is a Russian proverb quoted to Durward by Markovitch and Semyonov: "In each man's heart there is a secret town at whose altars the true prayers are offered." Semyonov has a secret reason for hounding Markovitch; Markovitch, a secret reason for committing suicide. Vera is afraid to acknowledge her secret—that she loves Jerry Lawrence. Bohun, who is also attracted to Vera, keeps it a secret. As in *The Dark Forest,* only

Durward—who keeps his nostalgia for Marie to himself—knows about them all.

His comments on Russia and the Russian character are thought-provoking, but he does not pretend to expertness: "This business of seeing Russian psychology through English eyes has no excuse except that it *is* English. That is its only interest, its only atmosphere, its only motive . . . any one's ideas about Russian life are of interest." This fact alone would not suffice to keep *The Secret City* in the permanent Walpole canon. However, the slow-moving narrative is ultimately compelling, Durward's tone is for the most part sincere, and there are a variety of interesting characters. Add to these its uniqueness—Walpole's eyewitness position vis à vis the events described—and I would rank *The Secret City* among the upper 25 percent of his novels.

III The Green Mirror

As I have noted, three Walpole titles, written before he went to Russia, contain characters related to Russia in some way. One is *The Green Mirror* (1918; U.S. ed. 1917), begun in 1913 but published after *Dark Forest*. Worried, in 1917, that the 1902-3 setting would seem "old-fashioned," Walpole prefaced the work with an apology: "We are now in a world very different from that with which this story deals. . . . But I will frankly confess that I have too warm a personal affection for Katherine, Philip, Henry and Millicent to be able to destroy utterly the signs and traditions of their existence. . . ." Except for Philip, these characters are cousins of John Trenchard of *The Dark Forest*. *The Green Mirror* centers upon Katherine Trenchard, the oldest daughter of conventional upper-middle-class parents residing in London, and upon her romance with Philip Mark, a thirty-year-old Englishman just returned from Russia. Why he went is not clear, but he was there "for years"; "knows Russia thoroughly"; and, it is later discovered, has had a Russian mistress. The novel shows what occurs when English middle-class morality (at least before World War I) encounters a man with Philip's seemingly amoral background.

The answer is that, barring accidents, nothing occurs! The man is ignored or, if that is impolitic, his background is. Using such tactics, stolid Mrs. Trenchard almost succeeds—in fact, she *does* succeed for a time—in foiling Philip's efforts to free her favorite daughter, Katherine, from maternal domination. Mrs. Trenchard's master stroke is her refusal to precipitate a crisis, even when she hears about the Russian mistress. Finally, the parlor mirror, the novel's main symbol, is broken. The mirror is green because everything it reflects—walls, carpet, curtains, the view through the windows—is green. Staring at it early in the novel, nineteen-year-old Henry Trenchard makes an unnerving discovery:

His people, his family, his many, many relations, his world . . . were all inside the Mirror—all embedded in that green, soft, silent enclosure. He saw, stretching from one end of England to the other, in all Provincial towns, in neat little houses with neat little gardens, in Cathedral Cities with their sequestered Closes, in villages with the deep green lanes leading up to the rectory gardens, in old country houses hemmed in by wide stretching fields, in little lost places by the sea, all these persons happily, peacefully sunk up to their necks in the green moss.

Later in the novel, when he hears that Philip, who has been kind to him and whom he admires, has had a mistress, Henry—moved by rage and latent sexual envy—hurls a book at his sister's fiancé but breaks the mirror instead: "There was a tinkle of falling glass, and instantly the whole room seemed to tumble into pieces, the old walls, the old prints and water-colours, the green carpet, the solemn bookcases, the large armchairs—and with the room, the house, and with the house . . . Trenchards and Trenchard traditions—all represented now by splinters and fragments of glass, by broken reflections of squares and stars of green light, old faded colours, deep retreating shadows." "Faded" and "retreating" are important words; for, after the mirror is shattered, Mrs. Trenchard's control of her children and her increasing control of Philip are shattered also. The smash comes when Katherine, realizing that Philip is gradually losing his grip, insists on an elopement. Mrs. Trenchard's refusal to see them again saddens Katherine but leaves her unrepentant. Henry, who has been kept at home by his possessive mother, is allowed to go to college—recalling *Maradick at Forty* and *Hans Frost*, where female liberation precedes male freedom.

The theme of *The Green Mirror*—that repressed youth should take matters into its own hands—seems even timelier now than then. The story line is believable, as are the settings. Diction and syntax are smooth; but the long passages that hash and rehash the lovers' problems make the novel as a whole extremely dull. Moreover, two of the main characters are unconvincing. The acts of Mrs. Trenchard, the strongest of Walpole's repressive mothers (Peter's mother-in-law in *Fortitude* is another), fail to fit her explicated personality. The author says that she is implacable and domineering; but, when he gives us her inner thoughts and lets her talk, she seems harmless. And so it is with Philip, whose Russian experience supposedly makes him a man of the world: his words and actions do not fit the role. His task in the novel is like Harry Trojan's in *Wooden Horse*. Harry, coming from New Zealand, breaches the "Trojan wall"; Philip, coming from Russia, breaks the Trenchards' mirror. Most readers find Harry's story the more entertaining.

IV *"Parables of the Time"*

Walpole's months in the "Sanitar," his directorship of the British propaganda bureau in Petrograd, and finally his employment by the Foreign Office in London kept him in close, official touch with Russia for about five years—from August, 1914, to February, 1919. The friendships he made in Russia and his admiration for Russian literature make it easy to see why Russia concerned him for the rest of his life. In 1919–20, on his first American lecture tour, one of his lectures was entitled "Russia." As shown by a headline in the *New York Times* (October 12, 1919) —"Walpole Sees Hope in Russian Common Sense"—his views on Bolshevism tended to be sanguine.

For the next seventeen years, discussing Russian writers was part of his repertoire; but "Russia" as a separate lecture was dropped after the first tour due to Walpole's growing uncertainty about Bolshevik methods. As the years passed and as the wheels of Leninism, then of Stalinism, ground on, he became more concerned. In 1925, when Dostoevski's daughter was in need, Walpole was the writer picked to send her appeal to the London *Times*. In 1933, he wrote a preface to *Out of the Deep: Letters from Soviet Timber Camps*, a bitter exposé of Siberia. He deplored, predictably, the Marxist proletarian novels of the 1930's, whether written in Russia, Western Europe, or America. For a time he even toyed with Fascism as a check to Communism; for, like many British intellectuals, he admired flamboyant Benito Mussolini. He held no special brief for Hitler, whom he met in

1925 at the Wagner Festival in Bayreuth; but, again like most of his countrymen, he admired Germany. Yet he was shocked to hear his conciliatory short story "The German" (1933) described as pro-Nazi propaganda [5] (an earlier story, "The Whistle," invites the same interpretation). Also upsetting was the formation in England of a neo-Fascist group, the New Party, which during its brief existence was supported by many important people, including Walpole's former Foreign Office chief, Lord Beaverbrook, and historian-biographer Harold Nicolson, a close friend of Virginia Woolf's.

As European affairs worsened and as the dictators went unchecked, Walpole's alarm mounted. His dismay can be traced through four novels, including the last one he wrote—*The Killer and the Slain*, published posthumously. On the other three he bestowed a secret label, "Parables of the Time," confiding to his journal (Jan. 7, 1939): "No one of course will ever see that 'Captain Nicholas' 'A Prayer for My Son' and 'The Sea Tower' all belong together and are parables of the Time—Nicholas, Colonel Fawcus, Bessie Field all analogies of the Dictators. *I* mustn't say so lest I be thought sententious." Never publicly revealed, the label is obviously a useful one.

Filled with references to the wobbly state of European affairs, *Captain Nicholas* (1934) makes a plausible "Parable of the Time." Like the original Fascisti, Nicholas Coventry is an intellectual; his favorite poet is the American turncoat Ezra Pound, resident in Italy. Nicholas and the eight-member Carlisle household (Mrs. Fanny Carlisle, the protagonist, is his sister) converge when Nicholas, debt-ridden and deported from Italy for certain vague crimes, arrives in London with his young daughter and an Italian bodyguard. Father and daughter move in with the Carlisles while the bodyguard holes up nearby. The bodyguard and the title "Captain" lend Nicholas a superficial air of military dictator; and the gullible Carlisles, representing overcomplacent Britain, become his puppets as he pries their secrets from them and sows general disruption. Most pitiable perhaps is ten-year-old Lizzie Coventry, who is caught between her jaunty, ruthless father and the kind but naive Carlisles.

Near the end of the story, when his aroused hosts evict him, Nicholas justifies himself: ". . . I thought it time you and Fanny were up against something that really mattered," he informs his brother-in-law. "Life's real, you know, full of rogues and sudden death. . . . Not at all the pretty sentimental thing you fancy it is. . . . Remember I've done you a good turn. You'll all of you go about the world now with your eyes a bit more open." In later Parables, Walpole becomes more severe with his "dictators"; but Nicholas, after his expulsion by his sister's family, is free to practice his insidious habits in other unsuspecting circles. That he is doomed to repeated ostracism unless he reforms is suggested by his surname, Coventry, however.

In a publicity blurb written for his publishers on May 25, 1934, Walpole ignored the novel's political side. Calling *Captain Nicholas* "a companion picture to 'The Green Mirror,'" he explained: "In 'The Green Mirror' an English family was dangerously invaded by a stranger. Mrs. Trenchard, the mother of the family, won the battle but at great cost. Now in 1932 . . . again [a] mother wins a victory. Twenty years have brought many changes into English family life, and the two books make, in this respect an interesting comparison." Putting aside the question of whether or not Mrs. Trenchard "won," Walpole was right in that Coventry, like Philip Mark, is one of his archetypal "strangers" whose coming unsettles things. But Philip—and Archie Traill, Harry Trojan, and Nathalie Swan—interrupt situations such as family smugness and petty tyranny that need interrupting because they are basically bad; whereas Nicholas' arrival and protracted stay influence for the worse something fine—a cheerful family circle and a happy marriage.

In tone, ideology, and plot complexity, *Captain Nicholas* is different from *The Green Mirror;* and it is also worse. To my mind, in fact, it is Walpole's worst work. The day he began it, he wrote in his diary (Dec. 24, 1932), "It seems a bit tame . . . but I daresay I shall soon get into it." He did, but tame it remained. The dialogue is trivial; the opening scene, charming in its presentation of Fanny Carlisle, is not assimilated into the plot, thereby missing an excellent chance to tie in at the end and enliven a perfunctory epilogue. And the middle drags. "Of course it's damn minor, *damn minor*," confessed Walpole to a friend. "Just hope I get by with it. That's all," he told his diary (Oct. 2, 1934). He more than "got by with it," sad to relate. An American Literary Guild choice, it was opted by David Selznick for William Powell and Shirley Temple (an incredible choice for Nicholas' fey young daughter); and in

England Leslie Burgess converted it into a play, which was poorly received.[6]

If *Captain Nicholas* was greeted more fervently than the other "Parables of the Time"—and with less reason—this was partly due to its "Time"-serving mode. Walpole in his Russian novels had handled microcosm-macrocosm congruities effectively, giving the microcosm in each case a tragic dignity. The word "Parable" suggests a similar approach, yet *Captain Nicholas* reduces important political issues to the dimensions of soap opera—but perhaps soap opera was the only mode possible. It is easy to criticize Walpole for not taking Fascism more seriously in 1932; but popular novelists know that their audience is conventional, and he was not writing a propaganda tract. His later responses—the bizarre psychology of *The Killer and the Slain,* the sadistic thread in the otherwise traditional *Sea Tower,* even the fairy-tale atmosphere of *A Prayer for My Son*—seem more adequate to the political situation.

A Prayer for My Son (1936) focuses on Colonel Fawcus, "a figure of greed and destruction," as Walpole later described him, "signifying my hatred of Naziism, or indeed any power that [is] aggressive, greedy, brutal towards weaker souls or altruistic, unselfish ideologies" (Cumberland Preface, vii). Fawcus, like Nicholas, has a military title; his surname is close to "Fascist," and he admires the Nazi book burnings and strict training of the young, which he practices on his ward and grandson, John—the young, as with Lizzie Coventry, bear the burden of their elders' experiments. The fact that John, with such a background, is spontaneous and trusting is a flaw in characterization. At the climax, the Colonel's four "prisoners"—John, his tutor, his mother, and his old-maid aunt—make their separate flights from the Colonel's fortress-like house in the Cumberland hills. "I intended the fantastic and romantic escape at the end to convey the sense that all of the Colonel's power was powerless so soon as you shook his dust off the soles of your feet," Walpole later explained. "It is, I wish to remind you, a modern Grimm fairy story" (Cumberland Preface, viii).

"Grimm" though parts of the story are, Fawcus is not an unmitigated scoundrel. Deserted by most of his household, attacked by lameness and beset by old age, he has started repenting by the end of the book. The heroine who arranges the mass escape, after her appeals to the Colonel's better nature fail, is Rose Clennell, John's natural mother. On vacation from her job with the League of Nations, her suggestion near the end that parlance is better than violence is what we expect. She is the protagonist, since "my" in the title refers to her. The theme underlying the "Parables of the Time"—that dictators are to be feared and must be over-thrown—places Fawcus in the subordinate role of antagonist; but his influence is all-pervasive. This presence of a strong antagonist at the center of the action—the same treatment accorded Semyo-nov in *The Secret City* and Mrs. Trenchard in *The Green Mirror* —is a terror-tale device closely related, of course, to the pursued-protagonist pattern.

While less popular than *Captain Nicholas, A Prayer for My Son* was kindly received. That its parable is more obvious was proved by a plaint from the *Times Literary Supplement:* "We had much rather not drown such a fresh and lively story . . . in . . . sauce from the dreary international tureen." [7] *A Prayer for My Son* is better structurally, the characters are more individual than in *Captain Nicholas,* and Fawcus is sketched more strongly than Coventry. Hollywood paid 2,750 pounds for the film rights (the movie was never made), and the Literary Guild chose it as an "alternate."

The text itself is marred by discrepancies. An open window is opened five pages later; a man who is standing rises from his chair; and so on. Ill during most of the time the novel was being written, Walpole dictated the first parts, a practice he abhorred, and composed the last in a health sanatorium. This illness explains Fawcus' rheumatism, Walpole's own problem, at the end. Worse than the punishment of Nicholas Coventry, Fawcus' sudden illness and awareness of old age were soon to be superseded, however, by the imprisonment meted out to Bessie Field in *The Sea Tower.*

Walpole's third "Parable of the Time," *The Sea Tower* (1939) contains few allusions to current political affairs. Once aware of its Parable status, we see in Elizabeth Field's first name an allu-sion to Elizabeth I of England, who is always pictured by Walpole as a ruthless autocrat (see *The Bright Pavilions*). A partisan of Mary Queen of Scots since boyhood and friendly in his later years to Catholicism, the author of *The Sea Tower* calls his young protagonist Christina; her husband's name is Joseph; and the climax, Mrs. Field's attack on Christina, suggests the threatened attack on Christianity by "godless, pagan" Fascism. Another symbol is the sea tower. Built in Norman days but still strong and beautiful, wreathed in opalescent mist, it represents England; and Mrs. Field, who has "always hated it," threatens to have it torn down.

Under a veneer of urban varnish, Joe is an easygoing, rather crude young man. At the end, he is more alert to the maternal, incestuous love that has enslaved him since boyhood; otherwise, he has changed very little. Christina changes a great deal, for the beautiful ingenue of the first pages is a sober, thoughtful matron six months later. Her chief teacher in these difficult months is the tower, whose calm strength and long history impart the message that the "discipline of experience" leads to adulthood. Christina passes this lesson along to the younger Field son, Congreve, an amateur painter. Bewitched by his sister-in-law's beauty and increasing goodness, he feels an upsurge of artistic power; frees himself from his mother; and, like Hans Frost, leaves home to create his masterpiece. Meanwhile, the suicide of a lusty old souse of a sea captain, shamed by Christina's purity, seems a gratuitous tribute to the young woman's moral stature. Its topical message may have been that, in troublesome times, self-indulgence is out of place; abstinence is the rule.

Structurally, *The Sea Tower* is worse than *Captain Nicholas*. The trouble lies in the last two chapters where what should be the peak scene is reported ex post facto by Christina in a letter to Joe—an evasion of the author's duty to present his climax first-hand. Moreover, the same tale is repeated in the last chapter, again by Christina in personal conversation with, again, Joe! The author meanwhile has forgotten his facts, so that some events are pictured differently. Walpole, who rewrote the climax at his publisher's insistence (a rare request from Macmillan), always worked badly under pressure. When his editor, Thomas Mark, suggested reversing the last two chapters—a good idea, since the first one occurs three months later than the second—he refused (Jan. 25, 1939): the book's close must not be too heavy. We are left, thus, with the spectacle of mad Bessie Field, confined to her home after attacking her daughter-in-law with a burning poker, being waited on hand and foot by her adoring husband, whose only desire is to lighten her imprisonment. In "Parable" terms, this ending seems to imply that Fascists should stay home—an innocuous solution, surely.

The rewritten pages, the closest of anything Walpole wrote to picturing Lesbian tendencies (here, those of Bessie Field), bothered some readers: a "positive orgy of red-hot poker, slipping pajamas and naked flesh," Graham Greene called it; "the physical explicitness is sometimes embarrassing—there are passages which would be erotic if they were not naive. . . . Then the style becomes wordy, unbuttoned and grotesque." [8]

Walpole, however, did not stop. He deployed deliberate sexual fantasy as the vehicle for his fourth and last Parable, *The Killer and the Slain* (1942). Reviews of it tended to be critical. The *Times'* description was perhaps the most judicious: "It is, all things considered, the type of novel he did best, for which he had most talent; . . . a craftsman's exercise in the macabre, the bizarre, the psychologically unaccountable." Harold Hobson, years later, recalled it as a "pit of quicklime. . . . Walpole began by writing about courage [in *Fortitude*], and he ended obsessed by panic." [9] This verdict seems extreme, but in the dark year of 1942 many besides Mr. Hobson probably found it hard to enjoy a work whose hysterical compulsiveness can be seen from Walpole's own comments as he wrote it: ". . . what a lot of nastiness and pity for my own nastiness I have in me! It's all coming out in this work . . . exactly like automatic writing. . . . Hypnotized by 'The Killer.' . . . It tastes *nasty*" (Journal, July 27, 1940, May 14, 1941; Diary, Dec. 23–24, 1940).

Protagonist John Ozias Talbot and his antagonist, James Oliphant Tunstall, are presented with equal strength. This feature and the odd premise underlying the novel—that one man, after killing another, may *become* the other—gain piquance when the story is seen as a "Parable of the Time." Talbot, who narrates the story, and Tunstall both live in a seaside village in Glebeshire. Talbot, a minor novelist, has always lived there; Tunstall, a successful painter, has returned after several years in London. Both are married, and Talbot has a son. The struggle is presented through sexual metaphor: if *The Sea Tower* is the most Lesbian of Walpole's novels, *Killer and the Slain* is the most homosexual. Talbot is a womanish man; Tunstall, his *doppelgänger* or "pursuer," is precisely the opposite—an apelike "man's man," a caricature of masculinity. According to Talbot, they were attracted to each other even as boys, Tunstall always making the advances. Returning to the village as a grown man, he resumes his sway over the uneasy Talbot.

Despite Talbot's protests to the contrary, Leila Tunstall strikes the reader as a silly sentimentalist. His own wife is named Eve. Coldly beautiful, she affects the same Puritanical garb as Bessie Field: black dresses with a touch of white at the throat. When Tunstall, who in addition has a mistress, Bella (the story's most unconvincing character), cannot interest Talbot in himself, he takes pleasure in arousing Eve. Talbot, suffering from unacknowledged jealousy of his smooth-haired, low-voiced lady-wife, who proves after all to be a hoyden, follows Tunstall one night and pushes him off a cliff. As with Markovitch in *The Secret City*, the pursued has become the pursuer. Then the strange metamorphosis begins. Talbot finds himself abandoning his femininity for the aggressive masculinity of the murdered man. He makes Bella his mistress, reawakens Eve sexually, and becomes Leila's confidant. As the change increases, everyone—especially Leila's brother Richard, a newcomer to the village—grows afraid of Talbot. Talbot glories in this fear and in the hatred his pro-Fascist statements arouse, statements formerly made by Tunstall. His aggressiveness builds until he finds himself one day about to do murder again, this time with a gun. The intended victim is Leila Tunstall's brother, Richard, a young man of feminine tastes —Talbot himself as he used to be. So Talbot commits suicide.

The last chapter, a letter to Eve from Leila describing the suicide in her sentimental fashion, resembles Trenchard's diary at the end of *Dark Forest* in its tone and form. Talbot's diction and syntax recall Durward's: simple, conceived in primary colors (in Talbot's case, to the point of crudeness), and hypnotically direct. The best of the "Parables of the Time," *The Killer and the Slain* is the one least likely to live—its emotion-based outpouring of allegory is too much the product of the London Blitz. Tunstall is equated with Hitler and Mussolini in their more animalistic aspects; and Talbot, finding after the murder that he is himself even worse, commits suicide rather than become a sort of super-Nazi.

This plot twist stems partly from Walpole's own doubts about his love for German letters and music (especially for Wagner, Hitler's favorite), his discounting of the *Führer* himself, and his former approval of Mussolini. These reflections, added to the Blitz and his nightmare of what life might be like if Germany conquered England, weighed heavily upon him. Hence *The Killer and the Slain* becomes an eerie climax to the "Parables of the Time" and to Walpole's final comment on the political affairs he had watched so anxiously and so long.

V *Envoi:* Joseph Conrad, *a Critical Study*

While in Russia training for the "Sanitar," Walpole wrote *Joseph Conrad* (1916), his first nonfiction work, a literary biography. Its relation to his Slavic interests is clear although Conrad himself, as a Pole, intensely disliked Russia. Its four chapters are "Biography," an impressionistic treatment of the three backgrounds in Conrad's life, Poland, the sea, and Britain; "The Novelist," a discussion of themes, plotlines, and characters; "The Poet," a discussion of Conrad's style, use of atmosphere, and philosophy; and "Romance and Realism," an analysis of Conrad's "determination to save his romance by his reality" and yet "extend his reality by his romance."

The most original passages are in Chapter I, where Walpole imagines himself as Conrad beginning to write; in Chapter II, ii, a comparison of the structure of Conrad's novels with a typical sea-yarn; in Chapter III, i, an analysis of three passages to illustrate Conrad's developing style; in Chapters III, iii, and IV, ii, a comparison of Conrad's "poetry" with Robert Browning's and of his zest with Dostoevski's.

Walpole displays occasional wit, as when he describes the publication of *Nostromo* as a serial in—"of all ironical births"— *T. P.'s Weekly,* where it "astonished and bewildered its readers week by week, by its determination not to finish and yield place to something simpler." The drawback of Walpole's method is its presumptiveness. Assuming, as he often does, what Conrad "must have thought" (the two did not meet until 1918), he risks ignoring what he *did* think. A glaring example is Walpole's assumption that the sea to Joseph Conrad was a goddess, the object "of lyrical and passionate worship." Having presented this idea twice in twenty pages, he quotes a passage from Conrad describing the sea: "He cannot brook the slightest appearance of defiance, and has remained the irreconcilable enemy of ships and men ever since ships and men had the unheard-of audacity to go afloat together in the face of his frown." Walpole's feminine ocean and Conrad's masculine one are quite different. *Joseph Conrad* down the years has been quoted, when at all, for its assertion that Conrad "hesitated" between French and English when he began to write and that his French mentor was Flaubert. In a letter to Walpole, Conrad protested both statements; but recent scholarship has affirmed Walpole's hunch, at least about Flaubert.

Today, when Conrad's genius is acknowledged, it is difficult to appreciate the pioneer nature of Walpole's study. Although Conrad had been writing since the 1890's, when Walpole signed the contract in 1914 to write his biography, he was just starting to be known. Walpole wrote the second book-length study of Conrad. Richard Curle's, the first (1914), was received less well by the critics. As an exploration of artistic aims, *Joseph Conrad* by Hugh Walpole ranks far below modern criticism. The interest of the work today is historical—an early appreciation of a writer whose importance, discovered gradually, is now secure.[10]

CHAPTER 5

Evangelist

I   The Cathedral

THE political events described in Chapter 4, centering round
the rise of totalitarianism, pertained to the temporal realm
of human affairs. But striking as Walpole's reaction to them was,
he acknowledged a deeper commitment to the spiritual realm,
inside or outside a church framework. Formative years spent in
the shadows of three distinguished cathedrals in different parts
of England—Truro in the southwest, Canterbury (the holy see of
the English church) in the east, and Durham in the north—had
opened his eyes to the mixed satire and pathos of relationships
between churchmen and townspeople. Anthony Trollope's novels
illustrated the value of such data to the Realistic novelist; while
those of Meade Falkner, a Durhamite, exemplified the Gothic
approach by describing cathedrals as gigantic, malevolent, supernatural creatures. When Walpole wrote *The Cathedral* (1922),
both influences were at work, especially Trollope's (Falkner's
looms larger in *The Inquisitor* [1935]). Less "religious" than some
of Walpole's novels, *The Cathedral* presents effectively the strains
and stresses in the life of a churchman.

The setting, the shire town of Polchester, has a personality of
its own—more than one, actually. Upper Polchester speaks
through what a bishop reviewing the novel once described [1] as
the "little group of ladies sufficiently well born to be admitted
to the exclusive circle of the 'Precincts,' the whole interest of
whose life [is] centered in the microcosm of the Cathedral."
Archdeacon Brandon and Canon Ronder, the protagonist and his
antagonist, are in touch meanwhile with less savory currents of
town opinion through immoral, smooth-faced Samuel Hogg,
owner of a pub in Lower Polchester. Most of the action occurs
in middle-class circles, however, where gossips like Ellen Stiles
and tale-bearers like Miss Milton, the librarian fired for being

rude to Mrs. Brandon, give Polchester society its aura of petty intrigue.

The cathedral itself is served in like fashion by what one reviewer calls "the gaitered bravos" [2] of the all-male board. Trivial politicians, they become embroiled in the crucial issue between Brandon and Ronder: what outside churchman should be imported to fill the important Pybus St. Anthony post? "I think all this Cathedral intrigue disgusting," Wistons, the most progressive candidate, bursts out during an interview: "Back-stairs intrigue and cabal." Canon Foster, frantic about Polchester's soullessness, considers Wistons the only man able to revitalize the diocese. These are crucial times for the church, Foster cries; and Ronder, in echoing him, states the novel's thesis: "We Churchmen should step forward ready to face any challenge, whether of scientists, psychologists or any one else."

The time in the novel is 1897; but in the early 1920's, when *The Cathedral* was written, church reform was again a burning issue among those disillusioned by the war and its materialistic aftermath. At the front of the novel is an unlabeled bar of music from Debussy's "La Cathédrale Engloutie": religion has foundered and must be salvaged. Polchester Cathedral, "the largest cathedral in northern Europe," sheer on its crag in fog and cloud looks like a ship afloat on high seas. The watery motif is emphasized as Walpole describes the interior on the morning of Queen Victoria's Jubilee: "The great bell dropped notes like heavy weights into a liquid well. For the cup of the Cathedral swam in colour, the light pouring through the great Rose window, and that multitude of persons seeming to sway like shadows beneath a sheet of water from amber to purple, from purple to crimson, from crimson to darkest green." The main interior feature is Bishop Arden's tomb with its blue marble shimmering in the dusk and a sea-green ring on the figure of the image. Henry Arden, the "Black Bishop," is a twelfth-century figure invented by Walpole. Black-bearded and phenomenally strong, he once "killed an ox with his fist." Like the famous Thomas à Becket of Canterbury, Arden was murdered inside the cathedral, but not for political reasons: his enemies hated him for his pride.

Six hundred years later, Brandon, also a large man physically, rejoices in the legend of Arden's aggressiveness and confidence in the unique power granted him (as he thought) by God. Archdeacon Brandon is subject to the same delusions: he considers himself God's partner-at-arms—" 'As one power to another,' his soul cried, 'greeting. You have been a true and loyal friend to me. Anything that I can do for You I will do.' " His son says of him, "He's gone too far, just as the Black Bishop did"; but Brandon himself never makes the analogy. Near the end, haunted by a "massive figure . . . something like himself, only with a heavy black beard, cloudy, without form," he fails to recognize it. On his final visit alone to the cathedral, he kneels by Arden's tomb, desiring reassurance. "An icy hand, gauntleted, descended upon his and held it," and he faints.

Of such an outcome Walpole forewarns the reader in the first chapter when he states: "There had descended upon [Brandon] this afternoon that special ecstasy that is surrendered once and again by the gods to men to lead them, maybe, into some special blunder or sharpen, for Olympian humour, the contrast of some swiftly approaching anguish." One of the first things we read of Brandon is that "Many of the Polchester ladies thought that he was like 'a Greek God.' . . . Six feet two or three in height, he had the figure of an athlete, light blue eyes, and his hair was still, when he was fifty-eight years of age, thick and fair and curly like that of a boy."

These overt emphases on Greek parallels cease; but the plot reminds us of them, as the Spirit of Progress, descending on Polchester in the year of the Queen's Jubilee, topples Brandon from his height and kills him. The Spirit acts through a mortal, Frederick Ronder, the new canon, suave, diplomatic, well traveled and well read, who arrives from London a few months before the Jubilee. At the finale a church-board sycophant invites Ronder to a levee to read " 'a little Shakespeare. . . . We thought of *King Lear.*' " The parallel between this most Grecian of Shakespeare tragedies and Adam Brandon, stripped of all he holds dear and maddened by the thought of Ronder, makes its mention symbolic. During the meeting (unfortunately overlong and recapitulative) at which Ronder receives the invitation, the Archdeacon dies, and the story ends.

The artistry of *The Cathedral*, Walpole's second best novel, lies in its drama and in its characterizations. When writing the novel, Walpole felt that he saw Ronder "almost too clearly" and Brandon "so exactly that it's . . . as though I were standing up too close to him" (Diary, June 4, 1920, Feb. 24, 1922). From this intensity the reader profits as the characteristics of both men come into play with dramatic results. Moreover, other characters—quiet Mrs. Brandon, who hates her husband; Joan, the ignored daughter, who admires her father, but when he needs her has fallen in love; Falk, the idolized son, who is expelled from college and elopes with Annie Hogg—are well depicted.

Critics have praised the novel's only example of unorthodox technique: the green-cloud sequence in Chapter I, Book II. At five on a February afternoon a green cloud emerges over the cathedral. A device to pinpoint the time, it also symbolizes reconciliation. The Brandons are scattered—the Archdeacon with his enemy, Ronder, the rest with their lovers: Falk with Annie, Joan with Johnny St. Leath, Mrs. Brandon with Preacher Morris. Each sees the cloud differently. Its color reminds Joan of "early spring leafage" (innocent youth, like her own); and the next moment Johnny tells her he's her friend. Falk sees the cloud through Annie's eyes, as a wonder and a mystery; and it draws them closer. The prosaic Archdeacon sees the cloud in merely physical terms; and it vanishes when he rejects Ronder's offer of reconciliation. Clairvoyant Mrs. Brandon perceives the cloud as rest and peace; but behind it an orange sunset burns, and the cloud dissolves when Morris pleads again that he loves her.

The book's structure is traditional otherwise, as characters are presented at the beginning and described one by one, inside and outside, before the action starts. In stories like this one, in which "tradition" is the essence of the setting as well as the crux of the plot, a slow start is appropriate. Some of Walpole's other novels —*The Green Mirror*, for instance—have difficulty picking up speed. But the slow start of *The Cathedral* is more than offset by its ensuing pace of unflagging dramatic event.

After a play called *The Cathedral* (1930), written by H. Old-field Box and based on Walpole's novel failed, Walpole rescued the story and wrote his own successful play. Despite several other tries, it was his only real stage success. The play omits Falk's romance with Annie Hogg, but it follows the novel almost exactly otherwise. Mrs. Brandon's elopement with Preacher Morris was a sore point with reviewers, as it had been with some readers. Why is not quite clear—was it considered a slander on the English church or on the English social structure? (Box's play had updated the 1898 setting to 1928, showing the religious theme's continuing importance.) Anyway, when the play changed theaters in London, Walpole was persuaded to exchange the shy Morris for a rather coarse Polchester attorney. The published version (1937) sensibly retains the preacher.

II The Prelude to Adventure

The Cathedral has the same relationship to the inner life of a pastor as *Fortitude* has to that of an artist. Both emphasize personal connections and social environment—with this difference: in *Fortitude*, the author does not reveal the thoughts of Peter that produce his fictions; but in *The Cathedral*, we share Adam Brandon's spiritual cogitations, whose superficiality is basic to the plot. *The Cathedral* was Walpole's thirteenth novel; and three of its predecessors, *The Prelude to Adventure* (1912), *Golden Scarecrow* (1915), and *The Captives* (1920), while far from its equal otherwise, are thematically more "religious."

Written in six weeks to fulfill a contract, *Prelude to Adventure* is not bad, considering its "potboiler" status: "clear-cut—no muddle," as Walpole described its style (Diary, Feb. 13, 1912). His only Cambridge novel, its scenes of university life are vivid, often amusing. Against this background Walpole, son of the Bishop of Edinburgh, raises two questions: Does God exist? If so, under what conditions would He seem most real to a young seeker after truth? In contrast to the quest of the protagonist, skeptical Olva Dune, Walpole posits that of the silly, rabbity deuteragonist, Bunning, who joins an evangelical group and invites Dune to its chapel. Despite the revivalist's power, Dune realizes that the God he seeks is not there. He yearns for spiritual knowledge, having committed a murder which he feels certain was witnessed by God. The first scene plunges effectively *en medias res:*

"There *is* a God after all." That was the immense conviction that faced him as he heard, slowly, softly, the leaves, the twigs, settle themselves after that first horrid crash that the clumsy body had made.

Olva Dune stood for an instant straight and stiff, his arms heavily at his side, and the dark, misty wood slipped back once more into silence.

The story of the soul-searching student murderer is not unique: Dostoevski's *Crime and Punishment* is the outstanding example.

But Raskolnikov's crime is premeditated; Dune's is not. Traditionally at least, English "heroes" do not brood and plot evil deeds. Hence the insistence of Miss Dane and Miss Steen that Olva's act is not murder but involuntary manslaughter, "a blow struck in anger"—"the thing which might just as easily have happened on the playing-fields or in a man's rooms, in front of a dozen people, instead of . . . in the chilled and dripping wood." [3] Using a form of the pursued-protagonist pattern, Walpole mitigates Olva's crime by making Mrs. Craven, his sweetheart's mother, a murderer too. Like him undiscovered until they confess to each other, she "murdered" her husband by withholding his medicine. Her excuse is that Mr. Craven, like the schoolfellow Dune killed, was "evil"; but the fact that Dune's victim had gotten a local girl—whom Dune hardly knew—pregnant and refused to marry her, seems hardly cause for manslaughter.

The novel covers in time about two months. Dune is more scholar than athlete, but his crucial encounter with God occurs on a football field in the final game of the season: a unique episode, surely, among thousands of fictional rugger matches! The scene begins conventionally: "The earth was humming like a top. . . . Never before had he been so conscious of the right to be alive. His football clothes smelt of the earth and the air." Gradually, Dune becomes more exultant: "It was as though something had said to his soul, 'Presently you will feel a joy, a splendour, that you had never in your wildest thoughts imagined.' . . . The very sods crushed by his boots were leading him to submission." The climax comes when, after tackling a man successfully, Olva falls, apparently unconscious:

He was on his knees alone, on the vast field that sloped a little toward the horizon.

Before him the mountain clouds were now lit with a clear silver light so dazzling that his eyes were lowered.

Above him was a great silence. He was himself minute in size, a tiny, tiny bending figure.

Many years passed.

A great glory caught the colours from the sky and earth and held it like a veil before the cloud.

In a voice of the most radiant happiness Olva cried—

"I have fled—I am caught—I am held . . . Lord, I submit."

* * *

The religious awakening of this self-sufficient youth was described in more secular terms by the well-known psychologist Carl Jung, who in 1930 wrote Walpole that *Prelude to Adventure* was a psychological "masterpiece." "If only such people had more often the chance to commit a decent murder," Jung exclaimed of Olva Dune, for ". . . minor crimes done by the right people have ordinarily a wonderfully harmonizing effect, a decided moral improvement" [4]—whether on the murderer or on society, Jung did not say. But it is evident that to Walpole, Dune *was* one of the "right people" whose acts of manslaughter might be called "minor crimes." And that such a person deserves to be judged by God alone, not by man, seems to be the novel's thesis.

Artistically, the best that can be said of *Prelude to Adventure* is that it is good entertainment. The first part is gripping. The dignified Dune and the "slob," Bunning, a satirical self-portrait, are both believable. But Walpole was still uncomfortable with his women characters; and scenes of stilted emotion follow the introduction of the female Cravens as Mrs. Craven's exhortations and example (cloistered in a dark room with her guilt, she is dying) lead Dune to bid his sweetheart goodbye and to embark on a penitential pilgrimage—the "adventure" to which this story is the "prelude."

As for God, He is constantly euphemized into "a Voice," "a Shadow," "a tall white cloud," images found in Wordsworth's autobiographical poem *The Prelude*, where Walpole probably found his title. This Presence takes on sinister tones when, quoting another poet, Francis Thompson, Dune imagines himself pursued by "the Hound of Heaven." There is also a hint that Dune's earthly father is a stand-in for God. With so many avatars for deity, the religious theme ultimately loses much of its force.

III   The Golden Scarecrow

The questions animating *Golden Scarecrow* (1915) and *Prelude to Adventure* are identical: "How real is God?" "What is God like?" He is real, say both novels, because He can be felt, heard, even seen—by certain people; but *what* is felt, seen, and heard depends upon personal need. The God vouchsafed to Dune is relentless, as He must be to bring an erring soul into line; at the same time, He is beautiful and the source of all rapture, thus lessening, presumably, Olva's need for his sweetheart, whom he feels he must leave.

The protagonists of *The Golden Scarecrow* are children, and to most of them God is kind, benevolent, and comfortable. A series of related short stories, *The Golden Scarecrow* takes its theme from Wordsworth's famous "Ode on Intimations of Immortality from Recollections of Early Childhood." To dramatize its lines—that we are born "trailing clouds of glory . . ./From God, who is our home," that "Heaven lies about us in our infancy," and that this happy condition lasts through early childhood but weakens as we grow older and ceases altogether when we enter school ("Shades of the prison-house")—Walpole depicts nine children, ages one through nine, from every economic class, living on March Square, London. We see them at home and at play, with friends and enemies old and young, and during visits of the "Big Man with a Beard." Invisible to adults, He is always there when the children want or need him. Sometimes He is needed but not wanted ("Thou best philosopher," Wordsworth describes a child, ". . . Haunted for ever by the eternal Mind, . . ./ A Presence which is not to be put by"). Pretty eight-year-old Sarah views Him with irritation; but there is an incipient streak of cold-blooded sadism in her nature that needs curing before she starts to school. Only 'Enery, the six-year-old lackwit, will have the Big Man with a Beard as a lifelong friend.

The portraits of the younger children are best, the older ones are stilted; and picturing the "Eternal Mind" or "Presence" as a big bearded man is regrettably trivial. The Prologue and Epilogue, featuring Walpole himself as "Hugh Seymour" at age eleven and later grown, are trite and sentimental. The Epilogue's theme, that the spirits of dead children watch over their earthly homes, has nothing to do with the Ode by Wordsworth. Still, to take the all-but-intangible thesis of a great philosophical poem and to treat it overtly, by anthropomorphizing its chief Figure and by making Him responsible for each climax in a cumulative series of stories, is a bold experiment. *The Golden Scarecrow,* despite its faults, is something "different" in English literature.

IV The Captives

From the naive mysticism of *Prelude to Adventure* and *The Golden Scarecrow,* Walpole in his evangelical role moved to the criticism of religious institutions, as we saw in *The Cathedral.* Before this, he chose as his main butt in *The Captives* (1920) the pentecostal church, its outward forms and the spirit which, he felt, animated it. Begun in 1916, *The Captives* has much in common with *The Green Mirror.* Both mix London with provincial settings. Both plots, concerning thwarted love affairs, feature youth in revolt against "slavery" to adults. And Katherine Trenchard Mark, as a minor figure in *The Captives,* befriends the protagonist, Maggie Cardinal (the upper-middle-class Marks and Trenchards earn their money in business and the solid professions; the lower-middle-class Cardinals and Warlocks survive on the fringe of the professions as preachers, teachers, and legal solicitors).

The Green Mirror is the better known novel; but Walpole, loving *The Captives,* with which he identified his own struggle to escape the domination of religious parents, attributed its unpopularity to its steady denigration of churchly environments (Cumberland Preface, viii). These environments include the drab country parsonage where Maggie lives with her drunken father, the local preacher; the pentecostal household of her aunts in London; the feverish chapel (similar to the one in *Prelude to Adventure*) where the aunts worship; the strained atmosphere of her lover, Martin Warlock's, home dominated by his father, a genuine believer and inspired evangelist who insists that Martin follow him in the ministry. And finally when Maggie, escaping her revivalist surroundings, marries a Church of England pastor, Walpole gives us a glimpse of his smug, arid world. "Down with all authoritarian religion" indeed seems to be the theme. But the unpopularity of *The Captives* is probably due to its grim atmosphere which is seldom relieved by light or warmth.

Recalling George Gissing and Thomas Hardy, this approach was more compatible to Walpole's active temperament than the languorous Jamesian mode of *The Green Mirror.* But many readers find the 474 pages in fine print of unmitigated grimness in *The Captives* hard to take or even believe. Maggie Cardinal has the tragic start of a traditional English Romantic heroine: after her lonely childhood in a Glebeshire village, she is orphaned and sent to her London aunts. Nineteen, physically plain and socially awkward, she is earnest to a degree that confounds and shames her elders. These are *Jane Eyre*-like trappings, and first-person narration like Jane's might have made Maggie seem less stolid and her lover, Martin, less indeterminate. As it is, the reader cares less than he should that Maggie, frustrated in her love for God and her love for mankind, and Martin, caught between untrammeled love and an equally untrammeled religion, are "The Captives."

Admirers of Thomas Hardy and the Naturalist school, on the other hand, will probably enjoy the novel. Distinguished by its wealth of detail and by the fact that, having established his mood, Walpole consistently maintains it, *The Captives* ranks for me among Walpole's dozen "best."

V Portrait of a Man with Red Hair

After attacking organized religion in *The Captives* and in *The Cathedral,* Walpole turned to contemplating other aspects of religious philosophy. Tongue-in-cheek perhaps, he began with the concept of Antichrist in *Portrait of a Man with Red Hair* (1925), one of his bizarrest works. Admirers of antagonist Frederick Ronder's liberal doctrines in *The Cathedral* who doubt the selflessness of his motivation will observe with interest that Ronder and Crispin, the "man with red hair," have much in common. Plump, with melodious voices and soft white hands, both have a passion for exquisite *objets d'art.* Ronder lacks Crispin's red locks, appropriate to an Antichrist; and he seems sexless, whereas Crispin's tendencies are clearly homosexual. Most significant, though, is their desire for power and their possession of the personal magnetism that insures it. Ronder controls within the established church; Crispin has moved outside all churches, appointing himself the terrestrial viceroy of a deity who expects obedience and confers punishments but never rewards, since the most exquisite reward is punishment.

Against this demon Walpole pits a unique figure: the only American protagonist in his thirty-six novels (there are several in his short stories). Charles Percy Harkness, a kind of J. Alfred Prufrock—with all this implies of boredom, bachelorhood, and cowardice—at thirty-five is tired of living. Touring aimlessly abroad, he meets James Maradick, of *Maradick at Forty,* in a London club; and Maradick insists that if Harkness wants to cure his ennui, he should go to Cornwall—specifically, to Treliss. "Do you *want* adventure, romance, something that will pull you right out of yourself and test you, show you whether you *are* real or no, give you a crisis that will change you for ever? Do you want it?" Unsure at first, Harkness decides he does—and at this point verity ends and fantasy begins.

The sequel has its humorous side, as one reader notes: Maradick, "having encountered a maniac [Morelli] when on holiday at Treliss," urges Harkness to go there also; and, sure enough, Harkness meets another maniac.[5] And just as surely, the meeting changes his life. Harkness encounters the wily Crispin; falls in love with Crispin's frightened daughter-in-law; is imprisoned in Crispin's castle-like house and tortured, mildly but enough to be convinced that he is braver than he thought; sees Crispin hurled to his death; and proves himself to be not only brave but also noble by delivering his ladylove to her childhood sweetheart— and all within twelve hours!

Portrait of a Man with Red Hair was first published in 1924 as a serial in *Harper's Bazaar* with the cautionary heading, "Written and Published for the Few Who Can Understand"—despite which many readers did *not* understand; and charges of "morbid indecency" were hurled at Walpole. The scene in which Crispin chains Harkness and his friends, half naked, to posts in an upper room and pricks them with knives, doubtless caused the most concern; but, when the work was published as a book the next year, most critics did not turn a hair.

Structurally irritating is Crispin's disposal by a deus ex machina, a faithful old servant, scarcely mentioned before, who breaks Samson-like (his eyes having been gouged out) from his pillar and hurls Crispin through a window to the rocks below. Also, partly because it started as a serial, the novel is overstuffed; its action, slow-moving; the dialogue, repetitive. Diction and syntax are unpardonably old-fashioned and the characters are flat: Harkness and Crispin, without being stereotypes, are treated as though they were.

From Harkness' viewpoint the theme of the novel is *Fortitude*'s, " 'Tisn't life that matters, 'tis the courage you bring to it." But Crispin is the showman of the piece, which suffers from lack of focus as theosophy and esthetics both vie for our attention. Crispin's lust for lovely bibelots, described with mouth-watering intensity by the author, has nothing to do with the theology underlying his melodramatic actions. Flabbily flamboyant like Crispin himself, *Portrait of a Man with Red Hair* is poor Walpole.

VI Harmer John

With *Harmer John* (1926), composed over a period of two years,[6] Walpole drew a purer breath and recorded a religion he could accept, a spiritualization of Crispin's selfish esthetics: the gospel of communal beauty. Those who beautify the world will revolutionize it (a more general belief today than when Walpole was writing). Hajalmar Johanson's ideal beauty, highly sensitive and society oriented, owes much to nineteenth-century estheticians John Ruskin and William Morris.

The half-Nordic Harmer John (Morris' special interest was Icelandic culture) leans, like Ruskin, toward Italy for the artistic inspiration he hopes to share with others. A non-churchgoer, he is drawn to Polchester Cathedral by the Brytte Monument, significantly a gayer sculpture than the formidable Black Bishop's tomb that inspires Brandon in *The Cathedral*. Although Simon Petre, who built the Brytte Monument, was a local artist, ". . . Mino de Fiesole himself would not disdain the babies crowding at the head and feet of the recumbent figure—the loveliest babies, some laughing, some grave, one with his finger on his lips, one looking back, calling to his friend, two bending forward, their chubby fingers on one another's shoulders—adorable, adorable babies making perfect the delicacy of the lacelike background, the strength and dignity of the simple figure, the symmetry and pattern of the wings of the guarding Angel."

A disappointed artist himself, muscular Harmer John is a masseur and calisthenics teacher. He ties his gospel of beauty into his profession by preaching exercise and muscle-building to make the body beautiful. From bodily beauty, beautiful homes, beautiful parks, and beautiful buildings everywhere will come beauty of the spirit (even paupers, striving for beauty, will abandon their slough)—then what may man not accomplish? Harmer John yearns to make Polchester (his dead mother's birthplace) what we would call a "model city"—a utopia for the world to emulate. It is long before he realizes that Polchester opposes him.

Although Harmer John belongs to no church and is not a Christian, he has a God. His God is Beauty; and his attempts to share this doctrine with humanity sanctify him. He is linked to Christ by his age (thirty); his date of arrival in Polchester (December 24); his sea clothes and carpentering talents; his handful of followers, including sinners and wastrels; his love for the sculptor of the Brytte Monument, Simon Petre; his healing powers; his refusal to flee death (at Samuel Hogg's instigation the rabble stone him and hurl him into the sea), and his predicted return. Too many allegories, however, have been based on the Christ story for Walpole's to seem especially new. Its reception disappointed the author, who regarded *Harmer John* as part of his own spiritual autobiography (Journal, Aug. 31, 1937). Especially daunting was the review in the *Times Literary Supplement:* ". . . it is very difficult to be effectively uplifting for nearly five hundred pages unless you have an unusual fund of moral intensity—the kind of moral intensity which Mr. Walpole has not, and which, having it not, he fails to convey to his hero."[7]

The minor characters are good. The deuteragonist, Maude Penethen, is one of Walpole's most vivid young women; his favorite type physically, she is small, light-footed, redhaired; and her love scenes with Harmer John are very fine. Psychologically believable, delicate yet passionate, these love scenes rank among Walpole's best. On the other hand, while the diction is natural and readable, the syntax is repetitive and slack. But the book's main fault, as the *Times* review pointed out, is Harmer John himself; unfortunately he is too colorless to arouse much interest or concern.

VII The Inquisitor

When Walpole's hopes for *Harmer John* miscarried, he abandoned for almost a decade his efforts to interest his readers in religion. Finally, he found a new background for the subject in the Canterbury Festivals which, in the early 1930's, began featuring an annual pageant (T. S. Eliot's *Murder in the Cathedral* is the most famous one) to dramatize the death of Thomas à Becket.[8] Walpole, whose ties with King's School, Canterbury, were still strong, decided to write a novel describing such a pageant. Since the gospel of secular beauty offered in *Harmer John* had failed to appeal, *ritual* beauty was perhaps the answer —if outside the church and if available to all.

The result was *The Inquisitor* (1935), Walpole's final Polchester novel. The pageant described commemorates the assassination of Henry the Black Bishop, Brandon's mentor in *The Cathedral*. The time is the Great Depression; and, by their huge expenditures, the pageant committee has alienated Polchester's poor, who threaten to riot on the crucial day. When the day comes, however, all classes are caught up in the splendor of the drama and their pride in the cathedral. The rifts are healed, temporarily at least; and Polchester is at peace.

Alongside this commemoration of a historic murder, a modern murder has been committed, exacerbating the town's nerves even more. It is solved when the murderer leaps to his death inside the cathedral after the pageant's conclusion. Meanwhile, there are signs that the cathedral itself is disintegrating. Despite the still grand exterior (the pageant is staged outside the front portal), those who know the building well are painfully conscious of its tottering spire and of its treacherous stairwells—down one of which, it is discovered, the rotting corpse has been stuffed.

Pertinent to the religious theme is the fact that—instead of the cathedral monuments, publicly available, that inspire Brandon and Harmer John—protagonist Mike Furze of *The Inquisitor* has a personal fetish: a black marble crucifix from Spain. Half-ashamed of his weakness for the Christus, Mike assures himself in alternate moments that nobody else could appreciate it. A real antihero, Furze is Walpole's most despicable protagonist; and his brother and antagonist, Stephen Furze, who redeems the crucifix from the shop where Mike is forced to pawn it, is the most repellent figure in Polchester. Their selfish struggle runs counter to the communal ritual being created before their eyes and in which they take no part. A miser and money-lender, Stephen cares nothing for the crucifix; he keeps it only to torment Mike, whose conviction that he is a Judas for having pawned the Christus, leads finally to Stephen's murder. The "inquisitor" whose omnipresence is assumed, symbolizes different things to different characters: Death (to Stephen); a shadow on the wall; God; the Recording Angel (to Ronder, Brandon's old enemy who reappears in *Harmer John* and finally dies in *The Inquisitor*). Mike imagines the inquisitor as Christ with a broken neck, an image neatly fusing his two manias: love for the Christus and hatred of his brother.

As Walpole predicted, this melodrama proved more popular,

even with reviewers, than the philosophical *Harmer John*. His own doubts (Journal, Aug. 25, 1935: "I don't care for any of the characters. . . . The book is . . . too grandiose") were mollified by the sales; but the end of his 1935 diary sums it up well: " 'The Inquisitor' my biggest success yet although far from my best book." Actually, the pace of the novel is slower than *Harmer John*'s. That the plot is more complex is not a fault *per se;* but the style sounds like that of a film scenarist (Walpole wrote most of it in Hollywood) who, after writing each scene many times, uses all his rewrites. Besides turgidness, its worst flaw is the unconvincing characters. Oddly enough for such lurid melodrama, they have more ink than blood in their veins.

VIII *Early Polchester: The Jeremy Stories*

One of Walpole's most likeable young characters is the hero of *Jeremy* (1919), *Jeremy and Hamlet* (1924), and *Jeremy at Crale* (1927). *Jeremy* itself has the added distinction of being the first book set in Polchester, soon famous as the background of *The Cathedral, Harmer John,* and *The Inquisitor*. On his fictitious shire town (Glebeshire county is between Devon and Cornwall [9] —where there is no actual "between") Walpole lavished so much care that many readers knew him solely as the author of the Polchester novels; indeed, to American readers especially, Polchester seems the quintessential English village. Wal*pole* and *Pol*perro (his vacation retreat in Cornwall when Polchester was invented) made the name inevitable.

With its street names changed—Lemon to "Orange" Street, Cheyne to "Rope" Walk, and so on—nearby Truro, his mother's home town, became Upper Polchester. The Cathedral is drawn mostly from Durham cathedral. For Lower Polchester, Walpole wanted a "Seatown" full of swarthy faces, which he found in Polperro. Crammed with the names of shops, streets, and people, *Jeremy*, especially in the last chapter, is a kind of Polchester directory. In *Jeremy and Hamlet*, Jeremy divides his time between Polchester and his first boarding school; and even at Crale, the young protagonist keeps in touch with Polchester through letters from his family, including the sympathetic uncle whose advice leads him to the most important step of his school career.

Walpole classified *Jeremy at Crale*, with its consecutive plot, as a "Novel" and the others, collections of stories, as "Books about

Children." *Jeremy* was written in Petrograd in 1916. "I told my agent last week that I thought I could do another children's book now," he wrote Mrs. Walpole ("another" alluded to *The Golden Scarecrow*); "as I could do a chapter every now and then as there was time, and it would be easy. . . . I'm to . . . do the stories when I like. It seems so absurd that I should get £1600 for a few stories I haven't shown them." [10] Because of this lax situation or because it was the first of the trio, *Jeremy* is also the most uneven. The best stories are "Christmas Pantomime," "Religion," and "The Merry-Go-Round."

Since "Religion" illustrates a trend in Walpole's thinking dealt with elsewhere in this chapter, let us consider it briefly. Like *Prelude to Adventure* and *The Golden Scarecrow*, "Religion" tries to answer the queries "Is God real?" and "What kind of God is He?"; and again the answer to the first query is "yes." In answering the second, *Prelude to Adventure* and *The Golden Scarecrow* picture a God of love whose strictness is confined to guiding errant souls. *Jeremy*, published four years after *The Golden Scarecrow*, contains Walpole's first portrait of the Old Testament Jehovah—jealous, fickle, cruel—who plays an important role in later novels. The religious doubts of *The Captives, The Cathedral,* and *The Inquisitor* rise from this concept; and it furnishes Crispin with his mad philosophy in *Portrait of a Man with Red Hair*— the farthest possible extension of the Commandment that says "I the Lord thy God am a jealous God."

In "Religion," distressed by the sermon his father, the Reverend Cole, preaches on Sunday about Abraham and Isaac at the mercy of a "God who apparently for the merest fancy put His faithful servant to terrible anguish and distress, and then for another fancy, as light as the first, spared him his sorrow," Jeremy decides to test God by praying for his sick mother. He enters the greenhouse with Hamlet, his dog, and starts to pray. A bolt of lightning and a terrible thunderclap bring him to his knees. He feels sure that God has spoken, particularly when he learns, later, that Mrs. Cole is better. But the image of an unloving, capricious deity remains with him.

Jeremy and Hamlet, which is consistently better than *Jeremy*, should be revived. It ranks, in fact, among Walpole's top fifteen works. The diversity of setting—Polchester (seven chapters), the country (two, both excellent), and Jeremy's school (three)—weakens it structurally; but all the stories end strongly, and the passages about Hamlet, the dog, are choice. In school, questions about friendship arise: What are its obligations, its dangers? What destroys some friendships, seals others? These questions, as vital to Walpole the adult as they had been to Walpole the boy (much about Jeremy is autobiographical), increase in importance in *Jeremy at Crale.* "The age of puberty is the terror of parents and head-masters," Walpole wrote later, in 1934 (Cumberland Preface, vii-viii); "no one dares to speak frankly, even in these frank days, of what everyone knows to be true. However, these are dangerous matters. I didn't write in *Jeremy at Crale* the school-story that I would like to have written, but I did . . . tell the truth so far as I thought wise."

Subtitled *His Friends, His Ambitions and His One Great Enemy,* the plot concerns the struggle—spiritual, psychological, and finally physical—between Jeremy and "Red" Staire, his "great enemy." The pictures of school life mitigate the harshness of those in *Fortitude,* based on the author's early, unfortunate experience at Marlow school, Buckinghamshire. In appearance and in history, "Crale" resembles King's School, Canterbury, which he attended from twelve to fourteen (Jeremy is fifteen). With its vivid football chapters, *Jeremy at Crale* should still appeal to young adolescents, although older ones will find it dated.

IX *More Polchester:* The Old Ladies

In *Jeremy,* Jeremy's uncle gives him a toy village for his birthday:

. . . six houses with red roofs, green windows and white porches, a church with a tower and a tiny bell, an orchard with flowers on the fruit trees, a green lawn, a street with a butcher's shop, a post office, and a grocer's. . . .

He would keep the village to himself, no one else should put their fingers into it, arrange in the orchard the coloured trees, . . . settle the village street in its final order, ring the bell of the church or milk the cows. He alone would do all these things. And, so considering, he seemed to himself very much like God.

Occurring in the first chapter of Walpole's first book with a Polchester setting, the message is clear: this is the way the author himself felt about Polchester.

Unlike some Romantics, Walpole never deceived himself that big cities symbolized Evil and the countryside Innocence. Polchester's bucolic charms are limited, as we have seen; and its physical features exert an unprecedented influence on its inhabitants, either for good or for bad—usually the latter. Critic Enid Starkie identifies this device as the "synoptic" concept in literature, naming Walpole as an outstanding example of pre-World War II writers who "saw a building, or a town . . . as developing its own personality, in which the individual members were of little account." [11] Such an aura, overemphasized, results in melodrama, as in *The Inquisitor*. Ten years earlier Walpole faced the same problem when writing the second of his "big four" Polchester works, the only one not about religion. Tauter, tenser, less ruminative than the other Polchester novels, in *The Old Ladies* (1924) the town's brooding atmosphere moves indoors and converts the upper-floor apartments of an otherwise empty house into a sort of hell. Experimenting with garish colors and sinister images, Walpole evokes a milieu most readers do not forget.

At its center is the villainness, Agatha Payne, with her startling gaudy-hued, gypsy-like *robes de chambre*, her olive skin, her jet hair and eyes. Like Crispin in *Portrait of a Man with Red Hair*, whom she resembles in her obesity and in her instinct for cruelty, Mrs. Payne loves beautiful objects; and this love is the motive and excuse for her crime against May Beringer. Crispin's adoration of bibelots is extraneous to the plot line of *Portrait*; Mrs. Payne's in *The Old Ladies* is not. (Both novels, incidentally, were dramatized successfully by other playwrights.) [12] This theme, the insurmountable lust of a person to possess a beautiful object, is peculiarly appropriate to Walpole, whose own passion for fine jewels and other *objets d'art* is expressed unrestrainedly in his diaries and journals.

Agatha Payne has a deep voice and a shadowy mustache. May Beringer, the thin old maid who lives across the hall, is sallow with popping eyes and a nervous giggle. Both are in their seventies, and the book's "shock value"—and its artfulness—lies in the fact that old-women characters can be as thrilling as young ones. The cozy title on the spine is no preparation for the lurid scene inside: a fat dark woman in a crimson wrapper lurking in an overheated room and willing a harmless old maid to die because she owns a beautiful piece of red amber.

To balance these murky effects, Walpole handles with tender compassion the third old-lady tenant, Mrs. Amorest ("silvery, delicate, like her name" [Steen, 141]). A penniless widow disappointed of an inheritance from a rich cousin's estate, she decries but is powerless against Agatha Payne's hounding of Miss Beringer. Mrs. Amorest's deliverance from the awful house comes, the morning after May's sudden death, through a successful son who returns unexpectedly from America.

"It is impossible to read the novel without making a vow . . . to treat helpless old people with more consideration," the popular American critic William Lyon Phelps exclaimed. But the contrast between sensationalism and sentiment poses an artistic problem. Which genre—horror story or sentimental tract—is meant to predominate? Like L. P. Hartley, some readers may find that "with such dangerous game afoot, the sympathetic analysis of Mrs. Amorest and her mundane fireside preoccupations [is] a little insipid." [13] Mrs. Payne is the bad antagonist; Mrs. Amorest, white-haired, refined, trusting in God, is obviously the good protagonist. But from my own experience I suspect that few readers the first time around even notice Lucy Amorest. By them *The Old Ladies* is probably valued as one of Walpole's stronger fictional efforts.

X *Envoi:* Anthony Trollope, *a Critical Study*

Before leaving Polchester, it seems appropriate to discuss *Anthony Trollope* (1928), Walpole's second critical study of a novelist. In *Joseph Conrad* (see Chapter 4), Walpole lent a hand to a living writer at a critical turn in his career; in *Anthony Trollope*, he helped revive an old mentor at a time when Victorianism itself was being unearthed and appreciated again. Because "Polchester" sounds like "Barchester" and because Archdeacon Brandon's quarrel over the Pybus question recalls one in *Barchester Towers* involving Archdeacon Grantly, some critics had called Walpole "a second Trollope" and *The Cathedral* "imitation Trollope." The parallels are superficial—"I am far too twisted and fantastic a novelist ever to succeed in catching Trollope's marvellous normality," Walpole stated gallantly (Cumberland Preface, vii-ix)—and the charge was soon hushed.

But no one was very much surprised when Walpole was asked

to write on Trollope for the English Men of Letters Series. He began on October 11, 1924; but he soon realized that, although he knew Trollope well, he would have to reread the fifty-odd novels to do a decent job. An American lecture tour intervened, and publication was delayed; thus Michael Sadleir's classic study preceded it, by less than a year. "It required a little courage, even in a writer of Mr. Hugh Walpole's distinction, to produce another monograph on Anthony Trollope so soon after Mr. Michael Sadleir's 'Trollope, A Commentary,' which left so little unsaid and said it so well," noted the *Times Literary Supplement*. "Mr. Walpole has nevertheless succeeded in avoiding the impression of either repeating or competing with Mr. Sadleir." [14]

This assessment was not wholly true. Walpole names Sadleir's study and Trollope's *Autobiography* in his Foreword, saying, "My debt to these two books, as any reader of this study will perceive, is immense, and must of necessity be so." In his next to last chapter Walpole quotes (with acknowledgment) paragraph after paragraph from Sadleir's work, published only months before! He may have meant to be scholarly, but it seems like a strange act for one who knew his subject so well. However, the *Times* lauded his efforts on behalf of the Irish novels, which Sadleir had ignored. Thinking Sadleir's study "better biographically than critically" (Diary, Apr. 24, 1927), Walpole strove for the opposite—except in the first chapter, where he lingered over Trollope's childhood, putting himself as always in the place of the unhappy boy.

There are strange anomalies in Walpole's style. Dignified and gracious in the first chapter, midway in the second chapter his tone changes. Cutting loose with gush and breezy clichés, the author sounds like fourteen, not forty-four. Such skittishness apparently stemmed from his belief that the Barchester novels, discussed in these pages, were a timeworn subject: "difficult though it is to say anything new about these books it is great fun to try," his diary reads (Sept. 14, 1927). "Perhaps I am being a little too colloquial but that will do the series no harm," he says blithely two days later. Harried by such expressions as "capital fun," "quite terrific," "perfect stick of a husband," "foemen worthy of her steel," and "too big for his boots," the reader may disagree.

With Chapter IV, Walpole rights himself; his style improves; and, after the derivative sixth chapter with its long quotations

from Sadleir, the last chapter is witty, informative, eloquent, saying much in a few pages. Reading it, we regret the earlier lapses
even more, especially the passages about Barset. Apt to be con-
sulted often, they give the book as a whole a bad image. At
the time, few critics seemed disturbed. But through the years, just
as Richard Curle with his work on Joseph Conrad soon overtook
Walpole as a Conrad authority, so Michael Sadleir with his continuing scholarship on Anthony Trollope has placed Walpole's
study in the shade—and deservedly so.

CHAPTER 6

Critic

MIDWAY between *The Cathedral,* the best of the Polchester novels, and *The Inquisitor,* the worst despite its popularity, Walpole wrote *Wintersmoon* (1928); and he won with it his first Book-of-the-Month Club award. *Wintersmoon* represents the apex of his London novels, called originally by him his "Rising City novels." Those "rising" are the youth of London; challenging the hypocrisy of the older generation, they make the city spiritually more livable. In *The Duchess of Wrexe* (1914), *The Green Mirror* (1917), *The Captives* (1920), and *The Young Enchanted* (1921), Walpole is all for rebellion; but by *Wintersmoon* he is less sure and he solves the problem wisely by having traditionalist youth confront rebellious youth on an equal plane. By the time of *The Joyful Delaneys* (1938), with war dark on the horizon, the phrase "Rising City" had acquired an apocalyptic meaning.

Of Walpole's eleven novels set mostly in London, five—*Green Mirror, The Captives, Hans Frost, Captain Nicholas,* and *John Cornelius*—are discussed in previous chapters. Although they take place in London, London is not their subject; but the novels discussed in this chapter could have happened nowhere else. London's geography, its social structure, and its heightened urban atmosphere are vital to their plots. Walpole emphasizes the areas familiar to him personally: Chelsea, Bloomsbury, Piccadilly from the Circus westward, Regent's Park, Curzon Street with its Shepherd's Market and Christian Science Church, St. James's Park, Portland Place, Baker Street, Hyde Park, Berkeley Square, Westminster. In or near most of these places he had lived; he could easily describe their houses, historical landmarks, shops, and clubs. The timespan of the London novels covers forty years, from 1898 in *Duchess of Wrexe* to 1938 in *The Joyful Delaneys.*

I The Duchess of Wrexe

"Dinner Lady Anna Chandos-Poole. Amazing early Victorian survival. Flaming wall-paper with crest—wonderful pictures—worsted flowers in golden screens. She hard old thing like one of Thackeray's women." This diary entry suggests an origin for his first London novel, *The Duchess of Wrexe*, begun two weeks later, December 24, 1912, and based on the "Rising City" theme. In the novel, nineteen-year-old Rachel Beaminster, living unhappily with her repressive grandmother, the Duchess, weds at her command an easygoing fellow in his thirties, Roderick Seddon (an upper-class Archie Traill), whom the Duchess herself fancies and thinks she can control—as proves indeed to be the case until Seddon, afer a near-fatal spill from his horse, is informed by the Duchess that his wife has fallen in love with a cousin. Seddon tells the old Duchess to mind her own business, and thus wins his wife's respect if not her love. She is carrying her husband's child, and the unfortunate cousin is kindly but firmly dismissed. Her last chance to dominate gone, the old Duchess turns her face to the wall and dies.

Unlike the settings in the later London novels, those in this novel are mostly interiors: the ducal town house (decorated *à la orientale*) in Portland Place; Zanti's antique shop (from *Fortitude*), where Rachel buys a silver bowl; the Bond Street gallery where the Duchess' portrait, which dominates the first scene, is displayed. (It seems natural to speak of "scenes": with up-to-date dialogue and chronology *The Duchess* would make a good play.)

Henry James, soon after its publication, assured Walpole that *The Duchess* was his best novel (Diary, Feb. 12, 1914). Six weeks later it was featured in James's famous article, "The Younger Generation," but in less glowing terms. "The squeeze pure and simple, the fond, the lingering, the reiterated squeeze, constitutes as yet his main perception of method," commented James.[1] The criticism, while apt, is ironic in situation, perhaps even intention; for *The Duchess of Wrexe* is Walpole's most overtly Jamesian work.

To put it bluntly—and to reduce James's own "method" to simplistic terms—*The Duchess* (like the later, more subtly Jamesian *Green Mirror*) consists of much conversation by many people about a simple problem of romance between the sexes. Late in the novel Roddy Seddon pleads with sympathetic Dr. Christopher: "Just drop all jaw about feelin's and such. There's been an awful lot of it lately." How completely we agree! Several characters giving the same facts in the same words after the author has explicated them—this quality justifies James's description of "the lingering, reiterated squeeze." James's own "squeezes," often "fond and lingering," were not "reiterated"; but Walpole failed to learn this "lesson of the master." The silver bowl Rachel buys symbolizes her fragile marriage as Maggie's is symbolized by a golden bowl in James's novel of that name; but the symbol is soon lost sight of—another "lesson" the young author had not learned. In later London novels, however, various colored bowls from Zanti's shop are used, and always to symbolize precarious emotions or situations.

Aside from the repetitiveness of which James complained, the style in *Duchess of Wrexe* is satisfactory, its traditional formalism appropriate to the late nineteenth-century society depicted. The main structural problem is the protagonist. The roles of Rachel and Roddy are merely pivotal, for the Duchess is meant to be the star. But the gap between the way Walpole describes her and shows her is too deep. In the past, supposedly, she was a woman of affairs, a great hostess, a wielder of destinies—a microcosm, in fact, of the ruthless Victorian Age. Her fate during the novel is linked with England's as it undertakes the disastrous Boer War—a war described by Walpole's mouthpiece, urbane Monsieur Brun, as marking the end of Victorian exploitation. After death removes the Duchess, the war tide turns in England's favor.

In speech and action, however, the Duchess is a petty shrew of no particular time or country—certainly not late nineteenth-century England—confined to domestic circles and devoid of the contacts she would certainly have had from the brilliant past Walpole gives her. "I had originally planned," he admitted later, "that she should remain, throughout the book, invisible, and I am sure now that she would have been more impressive thus" (Cumberland Preface, viii). Because of the Duchess herself, *Duchess of Wrexe* is a minor work, although in fairness I should add that most critics rate it higher than I do.

II The Thirteen Travellers

After *The Duchess of Wrexe*, the next two contributions to the "Rising City" group were *The Green Mirror* and *The Captives*. But, while much of their action occurs in London, their chief interest lies elsewhere: *The Green Mirror*, discussed in Chapter 4, is an instance of Walpole's early concern with Russia; while the milieu of *The Captives*—see Chapter 5— is the religious life, wherever encountered. Discussed also in Chapter 5 is *The Golden Scarecrow*, a book of short stories about a group of London children who are visited by a Supreme Being.

Equalling *The Golden Scarecrow* in structure but not in theme is the next book, *Thirteen Travellers* (1921), a series of short stories set in a specific London locale: comfortable Hortons Flats on Duke Street. No children live here, only adults; and their common tie is not religious but sociological. It is 1919 and each character is recovering from World War I, readjusting to society in his or her own way. One is Peter Westcott from *Fortitude*, still estranged from his wife, Clare; and the last chapter is narrated by Lester from *Maradick at Forty*, with whose wife Maradick, we recall, fell temporarily in love. Except for Lizzie Rand, a minor figure from *The Duchess of Wrexe*, the other "travelers" are new to us.

Like the children in *The Golden Scarecrow*, the thirteen travelers represent different ranks of life, from the portress at Hortons to its most affluent tenant. But the social attitudes are new. In *The Golden Scarecrow* "The poor ye have always with you" is taken for granted, as well as the superiority of the wellborn. By contrast *Thirteen Travellers* is almost Marxian. At least half the characters are seen in terms of the class struggle, the assumption being that public interest is moving away from the upper classes toward the lower.

The new attitude is given its most humanitarian interpretation by Hortons' wealthiest tenant, Tom Duddon, who says, "I don't want to pick and choose according to class any more. I don't want to be anything ever again with a name to it—like a Patriot, or a Democrat, or a Bolshevik, or an Anti-Bolshevik, or a Capitalist. I'm going by Individuals wherever they are." This statement might be regarded as the book's theme. Economically Duddon is contrasted with the Honorable Clive Torby, son of an erstwhile wealthy peer ruined by the war, who has to scrounge for a living. But Torby is young and survives. Absalom Jay, a relic of the 90's haunted by the spectres of "Bolshevism" and failing resources, does not. A gentle satire that never falters, his story, the first in the book, is the best.

In the chapter on Westcott, the literary circle of Katherine Mansfield and Middleton Murry is satirized when Westcott visits the studio of "Murdoch Temple," reads a "modern" poem which he doesn't understand, is scorned by a young woman "directed apparently by Temple," and leaves in disgust. "Let off some of my favorite antipathies which same did me a lot of good but I'm not at all sure it's proper art," Walpole's diary says (Aug. 29, 1919). After leaving the studio, Peter cheers up as he crosses Piccadilly Circus and reflects that London is "a nursery" and that "the wisest man alive knew just as much as his nursery-walls could show him." These pages, with their sanely whimsical tone, provide a good ending for an otherwise rambling story.

Despite the contemporary background, most of the plots are traditional. Topical matters taken up include Spiritualism (in "Mrs. Porter and Miss Allen") and the replacement of career women by returning veterans (in "Fanny Close" and "Lois Drake"; Lois, a returned officer herself, is denominated "the third sex"). Except for its weak close, "Mrs. Porter and Miss Allen" is arresting, for it is in the tradition of Henry James's *The Turn of the Screw*. "Miss Morganhurst," who weathers the death in battle of her favorite nephew with apparent calm only to go mad when her pet dog is killed, is praiseworthy as a case study. Outside these stories, "Peter Westcott," and "Absalom Jay," Marguerite Steen's comment (190) that "The magazine inspiration is evident" is all we need say about the rest.

III The Young Enchanted

In Chapter 2, I noted Walpole's predilection for the pursued-protagonist plot, where the protagonist is "pursued"—that is, followed, physically or metaphorically—or thinks he is. The pursuer may be the antagonist or the deuteragonist, depending on the mood and intention of the plot. Walpole's first three novels, we noted, *The Wooden Horse, Maradick at Forty*, and *Perrin and Traill*, employ the pattern; and we have had occasion to mention it since. In the London novel *The Young Enchanted* (1921), which is a superb example of this approach, so vital is the relationship between pursued and pursuer that we have really two protagonists. Brother and sister, they are Henry and Millie Trenchard from *The Green Mirror* (a decade younger than they should be, judging by the time of the earlier work), and their adventures, occurring simultaneously, are recounted in alternate chapters.

The theme again is the "Rising City," Walpole's aim being, he said later, to prove "that for the young men and women of 1920 the world in front of them should be more adventurous than the world behind them" (Cumberland Preface, xi). The action occurs entirely in London (not in one area, but all over the city), where the two protagonists spend much of their time trying to outguess their elders. Their mother, repressive Mrs. Trenchard, dies midway through the story, still refusing to forgive her older daughter, Katherine, for marrying Philip Mark. Both Henry and Millie are with their mother when she dies; but usually their paths run separately—with surprising parallels as both get secretarial jobs, both fall in love, and so on.

Several Walpole novels employ strong second figures, amounting almost to two protagonists; but none does it so systematically as *The Young Enchanted*. And nowhere else are the two plots so deliberately echoic. Henry's story, however, is essentially "romantic"; Millie's, "realistic." This distinction, plus the fact that the actions of one ape those of the other, recalls *Maradick at Forty* in which Tony's story is "romantic"; Maradick's, though similar in detail, "realistic." *The Young Enchanted* seems a deliberate successor to *Maradick*; in fact, not once in the decade after 1910 does Walpole pick up the gauntlet thrown down with the failure of *Maradick*—until, in his first postwar novel, he returns to the challenge, faces up to it, and (some would say, at least) wins. Henry's story, lighthearted in tone, improbable in concept, owes much to Tony's. There is the same rescue of a girl from her cruel parent; although Tony gets the girl, Henry releases his to another lover. As a character, Tony is less believable than Henry, whose super-Romantic venture fits his disjointed, chivalric personality, as already seen by us in *The Green Mirror*. His gallant rescue of the girl who loves somebody else and sails away, leaves him nostalgic but unscarred—still the "young enchanted."

Meanwhile, Millie's romance, fostered by an unprincipled female employer, ends much like Maradick's, in a salutary letdown.

Tempted to try an earthier relationship with the fiancé she ideal-izes, warmhearted Millie breaks with him when she learns he has deserted a pregnant girl. Deeply disillusioned, her pattern now the reverse of Henry's, she is no longer a "young enchanted." Near the end, she marries Peter Westcott, a middle-aged widower now.

Some readers may find *The Young Enchanted* frustrating; tired of chapter openings of the "Meanwhile, back at the ranch" type, they may wish the story were either Henry's or Millie's—either frothily Romantic or sociologically Realistic. *The Young En-chanted* is an interesting tour de force; conceding that, readers must then decide for themselves. Diction and syntax are fair; Henry's story, while humorous, needs more verve. A satirical pas-sage that describes a literary party he and Peter attend includes acid portraits of "The Three Furies" (Katherine Mansfield, Vir-ginia Woolf, and Rebecca West) and of "Campbell" (Walpole himself), hearty, red-faced and optimistic. But beside Millie, Henry, and perhaps Peter, all the other characters are shadows.

IV   Above the Dark Circus

The Young Enchanted opens in Piccadilly Circus, where Henry first sees the girl he follows home and later rescues. "All his life after he would remember that moment, the soft blue sky shredded with pale flakes of rosy colour above him, the tall buildings grey and pearl white, the massed colour of the flowers round the statue, violets and daffodils and primroses, the whir of the traffic like an undertone of some symphony . . . the warmth of the Spring sun and the fresh chill of the approaching evening, all . . . were, in retrospect, part of that wonderful moment. . . ."

Starting at the Circus, *The Young Enchanted* in 1920 moves freely around the city. A decade later *Above the Dark Circus* (1931) is confined within a half mile square, with the Circus as its focal point. The Circus itself has not changed; but the narrator, a jobless war veteran, sees it differently one December evening in 1925:

. . . the centre of the Circus was sinking into a dusk that resembled to my heated gaze the gray waters of a pool, and I had the fancy that omnibuses charging up the hill from the Mall, circling round from Piccadilly, were uncouth and barbarous monsters plunging to the pool for a savage drink.

. . . A moral world? It had ceased to exist for me, and in its room there was this strangely beautiful evil place, shot with coloured lights that broke and flashed and trembled across the sky above my head, while at my feet there were these strange sluggish waters, iridescent, cleft by monsters, bordered by walls of grim gray stone.

This mood picture fits the "Rising City" theme, which is no longer rebellion by youth. What is "rising" is the grim tide of the "have-nots," the unemployed. In *Thirteen Travellers*, immediate postwar social shifts were handled benignly under the assumption that the lower classes at least had jobs and would keep out of mischief. But the tone of *Above the Dark Circus* (American title, *Above the Dark Tumult*) is defiantly egalitarian as the narrator, Dick Gunn, fighting for identity as much as for life, reveals the temptations of the starving, whatever their social class.

The novel exemplifies again the pursued-protagonist, or "doubles," pattern—in triple form! The protagonist, Dick Gunn, to a certain extent follows the deuteragonist, John Osmund. Before World War I, both were enamored of Helen Cameron. She married Osmund, and Gunn joined the army. Now, early in the novel, they meet again; and Gunn learns that Osmund is mistreating Helen. Anger, mixed with curiosity—he had always admired Osmund—keeps him at Osmund's side for the rest of the evening (the entire action occurs in about ten hours). Gunn is present when Osmund murders Leroy Pengelly, an unsavory stoolpigeon because of whom Osmund had spent two years in jail for burglary before the war. The murder, by strangling, is unpremeditated; and Gunn helps Osmund dispose of the body.

An hour later there is a knock at the door of Osmund's flat above Piccadilly Circus and the visitor announces his name: Pengelly, Joseph Pengelly, Leroy's brother (the pursuit device again). Physical opposites—Leroy wiry and black-haired, Joseph chubby with glasses—the brothers hate each other; but a psychic affinity exists between them. Both are blackmailers: Leroy by profession; Joseph when opportunity offers, as it does now. Osmund is almost as strapped as the penniless Gunn; in any case, he's determined not to pay. In a rage, he chases Pengelly, terrified now for his life (Osmund is six-feet-six, and both the Pengellys are small), onto the street and into a nearby movie house. With wry recognition of the situation's oddness, the narrator recalls "the moment when, myself pursuing Hench [Osmund's bodyguard], I saw first little Pengelly, then Osmund and Helen, vanish, to my amazement, into the gallery entrance of the Trafalgar Theatre. . . . it was all I could do, I remember, not to break out loud into hysterical laughter. . . . What incredible farce was it that we were now playing?" But the convoluted pursuit presages no farce. Minus Hench, it continues to the rooftop, where Osmund, with Pengelly in his arms, leaps over the side to death.

This London "thriller" equals Walpole's Russian tales in its successful use of first-person narrator. Except for the end, where the diction waxes effusive, the tone is simple and direct. Narrator Dick Gunn is impatient, even brutal, because hunger and cold have made him so. Among Walpole protagonists, Gunn's chip-on-the-shoulder desperation is unique. He admires the Osmunds of this world, who are big and strong enough to dispose of the "little rats," yet he considers himself an idealist. His talisman is a set of *Don Quixote* bound in red.

Another rare figure is Osmund, the deuteragonist. Our inclination to like him is leavened, as is Gunn's, by the inclination to distrust him—an instinct confirmed by the story's final holocaust. In any other Walpole novel, Gunn or Osmund—one a murderer, the other his accessory—would be the villain; here the despicable Pengellys fill that role. Murder is set almost at naught while "squealing" and blackmail become punishable by the direst means. We recall Dune's unpunished crime in *Prelude to Adventure;* but, far from seeking God, Osmund courts perdition by destroying himself along with his victim.

Better written than the other "thrillers" it resembles *(Killer and Slain* and *Portrait of a Man with Red Hair), Above the Dark Circus* should be kept in print. Although returned soldiers seldom go hungry now, their problems are still with us; and an adventure like Gunn's, persuasively recounted, is entertaining anytime.

V The Joyful Delaneys

Above the Dark Circus was written just before the 1929 Crash. It was pure writer's luck that, when published in 1931, its desperate mood reflected the public's as the worldwide Depression, grabbing hold, began to bite. Six years later, *The Joyful Delaneys* (1938) grew directly out of the current scene. People, like the Delaneys, were still in need; they were also made nervous by the hovering clouds of World War II, and the "Rising City" metaphor becomes the "Exploded City" by the end of the novel as the imminent rain of bombs is contemplated.

Yet the title is not ironic. Those who knew Walpole well or heard him lecture, saw a humorous, lively side too seldom revealed in his novels. When a friend in 1936 asked him to write something "happy," he thought of the Delaneys—"the English aristocracy in their new poverty. *Exactly* the subject for me. But a *happy* book?" he mused (Journal, October 13). "But the Delaneys *are* happy: they can't help themselves. They are telling me now: 'If you don't portray us truly as we are, by God we'll torture you for ever.' And, God helping me, so I will!" The result of this vow was a diversion as quaint as its title, one appropriate for ladies-club reviews but of practically no artistic value.

Except for the reviewers in *The New Yorker* (anti-) and in *The Spectator* (amazingly pro-), most critics were undecided. "It is by no means everybody's novel, but it is certainly the work of a novelist," the *Times* asserted cautiously; "for he can bring together plots and figures, draw scenes, . . . and pour over all his many-coloured, romantic and effectual shower of words"; "romance vanishes when the magic lantern is turned off and the blinds drawn up, and so it is useless to bring into the open . . . these [characters] who function so smoothly and so beautifully within the pages of the book." [2] To "bring them into the open" was, of course, Walpole's last intention in escape fiction like the *Delaneys*.

The super-Romantic plot should be familiar to us by now: the rescue of one's beloved from a scoundrel. The Delaney son is the rescuer; the beloved is Lizzie Coventry, whose scoundrelly parent, of course, is Captain Nicholas (minus his former political connotations, presumably). Meanwhile, an elderly, indigent male friend of Mrs. Delaney's, threatened with violence by his ape-like landlord, tries to commit suicide. Much else is happening, for Mr. and Mrs. Delaney themselves have marital qualms and distractions. Their daughter's involvement with a young man who works in Zanti's antique shop constitutes a Realistic subplot. And the whole family is suffering from the Depression and the threatened loss of their lovely old home.

But everything ends well. Lizzie's worthless father releases her. Meg's elderly friend moves in with the Delaneys and is nursed back to happiness. The Delaneys' man-of-all-work follows his young master's footsteps and rescues his own love by punching her aggressive suitor—the apelike landlord, of course—in the nose. The daughter abandons her ambivalent relationship. And a deus ex machina—Lord Ragadoon, a wealthy old connoisseur—skips shamelessly forward, converts their house into an art museum, and makes the Delaneys the resident curators.

The lovely old house—a microcosm of the nation—is threatened with destruction (by bulldozers), but Lord Ragadoon gives his assurance that it's safe for at least another year. However, doubts about the national scene continue. The Delaneys attend, en masse, "the last great London ball" (presumably before The Deluge), given by the new, young Duchess of Wrexe, the daughter of a farmer. From the sidelines, Meg's nervous brother-in-law protests, "One has a kind of Brussels-before-Waterloo feeling, hasn't one? England's being so fine and noble. She doesn't want *anything* from anybody. Why *will* other countries be so selfish and grasping? Well, of course, she doesn't because she's *got* everything. For years and years she's had the world in her pocket. But the world's in her pocket no longer. Everyone thinks now they'll have a little bit of what England's got. How's she going to deal with it?" From these plaintive cries, it is clear why Walpole wrote in his journal, Feb. 14, 1938, "After the Delaneys I won't do a London novel again for a long time." In 1941, ten weeks before he died, he listed a new novel, *Meg Delaney*—but for 1945.

VI   Wintersmoon

In contrast to the lighthearted *Delaneys*, two earlier London novels were intended as serious studies of upper-class, urban society. In the first, *The Duchess of Wrexe*, Walpole's awkward handling of the milieu revealed that he did not understand it. Fourteen years later *Wintersmoon* (1928), one of his best novels, shows how much he had learned. The sureness of his psychology as he moves among people whose type he has come to know so well is matched by a new suavity of style, one as smooth as cream that is appropriate to the setting. The novel's only problem is pace, a bit too slow to give the plot developments the excitement they deserve.

The first three pages, a disembodied dialogue fascinatingly unlike anything else in Walpole, set the novel's tone. The speakers are a man and a woman; the conversation is a proposal and an acceptance. Her name, "Janet," is spoken once; his, not at all; and their passionless objectivity resembles the event: the betrothal of two people who are not in love. Wealthy Wildherne Poole wants a son, and Janet Grandison wants money to educate her sister Rosalind properly (Rosalind, ironically, is repelled by the money).

Wintersmoon marks the nadir of Walpole's faith in the "Rising City." Until now he had used the phrase to mean the rallying of London's youth to the banner of independence. But, between *The Young Enchanted* (1921) and 1924, when he began *Wintersmoon,* he developed a new *bête noire:* the generation of post-war writers whose effect on contemporary morals he feared (or thought he did). If youth followed their lead, if "Rising" now implied the overthrow of all moral restraint, Walpole could not support it. Especially alarming were the iconoclasm and immorality discernible, he felt, in the work of Aldous Huxley, James Joyce, D. H. Lawrence, the Bloomsburyites, Rebecca West, and Dorothy Richardson. "Selfish hedonism" seemed to him to be their philosophy.

This philosophy is expressed in *Wintersmoon* by the deuteragonist, Rosalind Grandison. It is no accident that Rosalind and Tom Seddon (the son of Rachel and Roddy from *The Duchess of Wrexe*) live, after their marriage, in Bloomsbury. Rosalind is opposed, not by the older generation (in this novel, an unusually attractive bunch) but by her sister, the quiet, tradition-loving Janet. Against Bloomsbury is posited Wintersmoon, the Poole family's lovely estate, symbolic of the enlightened traditionalism Walpole felt best suited England. That this stance ran counter to prevailing intellectual currents endeared Walpole to most readers. "I'm inundated with letters begging me to write 'Wintersmoons' endlessly," he told his publishers.[3] Later he described its popularity as a triumph over "the formless novel of ideas that was from 1925 to 1930 all the intellectual rage" (Cumberland Preface, xi).

But critics too were favorable. The author's "outlook [on] the tangle of postwar customs and morals . . . is what we should expect of him—urbane and sensible," the hard-to-please *Spectator* declared; "Mr. Walpole has long been a master of his craft, but in this book he excels himself." A more critical reviewer invoked the ghost of William Thackeray: "It would be gross flattery to

describe Mr. Hugh Walpole as a 20th-century Thackeray or . . .
'Wintersmoon,' as a new 'Vanity Fair.' But he is an apt and gifted
disciple of Thackeray, and as a novel of national psychology and
manners his story of the 1920s, is not unworthy to go in the same
gallery, if it cannot be hung on the same line." [4]

Several features in *Wintersmoon* link the novel with *The Duchess of Wrexe*. Lady Anna Chandos-Poole, we recall, modeled for
the Duchess; and Janet's husband is a Poole. Her vision of a rose-
colored bowl in Zanti's shop echoes the silver bowl Rachel Seddon
buys there; and both marriages, though for different reasons, are
precarious. Finally, Rachel's story ends in *Wintersmoon* after
Tom, her son and Rosalind's husband, commits suicide. "Tom was
cursed," Rachel informs Janet, "as I all my life have been cursed.
. . . And my grandmother knew it. She knows it now. . . . She
has been waiting for this for so long. At this instant how delighted she must be!"

Rosalind, after Tom's suicide, leaves London for Cumberland
with her lover, a dissolute, cynical, best-selling author. Janet and
Wildherne's attempts to get them to return are in vain. The
gauntlet has been flung. "There's Wintersmoon waiting for us.
Wintersmoon that Rosalind and her world are going to pull down,
and that we and our world are going to create new beauty from
—if we can. There'll be a struggle," Janet tells Wildherne on
the last page of the novel. (After three years of marriage and the
death of their baby son, they have finally fallen in love.)

Neither the plot nor the characters makes *Wintersmoon* the
champion of the London novels. For its supremacy we must thank
the language; stately and gracious, it fits the story's theme, the
value of gracious living, and its rhythms are such that the reader
finds whole sentences lingering in his mind.

VII *Walpole as Anti-Intellectual*

Masked as social analysis, the plot of *Wintersmoon*, as we saw,
stemmed partly from Walpole's distrust of writers like Aldous
Huxley, James Joyce, and the Bloomsburyites who were setting
the current literary world on its ear. In other books laid in London—*The Young Enchanted, The Thirteen Travellers*, and *The
Joyful Delaneys*, as well as in *Captain Nicholas, Hans Frost*, and
John Cornelius—he satirized certain fictionists individually, sometimes parodying their products. His first notes for *Wintersmoon*

were made in 1921, after the publication of Huxley's novel *Crome Yellow* and of Strachey's debunking biography *Queen Victoria*. 1922 was the *annus mirabilis* of Joyce's *Ulysses* and T. S. Eliot's *The Waste Land. Antic Hay* by Huxley and *The Dove's Nest* by Mansfield highlighted 1923. During the actual composition of *Wintersmoon*, 1924–26, Huxley's *Barren Leaves* and *Two or Three Graces* emerged, as well as D. H. Lawrence's blood-lusty *Plumed Serpent*. Walpole of course read all these and more.

His reviewing duties, if nothing else, would have kept him abreast of the New Fiction. Readers unacquainted with his extensive critical output may be interested in this posthumous comment in the *Manchester Guardian:* "Walpole was a balanced critic who seemed to have read everything. . . . He made extraordinarily few mistakes in his appraisements." Throughout his career, except during World War I, he wrote book columns and reviews regularly for magazines and newspapers on both sides of the Atlantic.[5] No more the "New Criticism" than his fiction is the "New Fiction," his critical assessments followed no system. The catholicity of his tastes caused him to laud many whom we today would not; but he had a healthy admiration for genius of the past, and he was quick to divine new talent. (See Chapters 4 and 5 for the discussions of *Joseph Conrad* and *Anthony Trollope*.)

Chatty, personal, unscientific, his kind of criticism is frequently called "appreciation." With its emphasis on spontaneity, this type of criticism is more widespread, even today, in Britain than it is in America (oddly enough, since many of the outstanding New Critics have been British). One of its main functions is evaluation: is a specific work good or bad? worth reading or not? Our tendency to avoid "value judgments" would puzzle Walpole. Once a critic's special bias was understood, he was expected to save the time and money of his readers by directing them to the right books.

When judging poetry (his drama criticism deals with performance only), Walpole limits himself to two aspects, the ethical and the vaguely esthetic. To prose, especially fiction, he gives a far broader treatment. "Hugh Walpole knows more than any other practising writer," fellow-writer and critic L. A. G. Strong stated, "and as much as most scholars, about the history of the novel." [6] The critics Walpole admired most, Sainte-Beuve, for instance, had used a biographical approach, relating the author's works to his life and times; and, when space allowed, Walpole followed their example. Some was mere literary gossip, but he told it interestingly, fusing to the mass of detail his enthusiasm for all who promote creativity. His voracious reading and almost photographic memory furnished the bibliographical tools: titles, dates, plots, authors, settings, personalities. He treated neither literary theory nor literary history profoundly: the "gentleman critics" of his era cultivated a light touch. But the facts at his fingertips lent substance to the body of tenets he preached and (if not always successfully) practiced.

Since novels predominate in his own output, it is useful to recall his ideas of what a novel should be. First, it should create memorable characters. He writes of Sir Walter Scott, for instance, that "It is in fact exposition of character . . . that is his greatest gift. This it is that makes him able to present with perfect truth a king, a peasant, a town burgher, a Prince of the blood, and to show them in the real human condition. . . . He does not hear, he overhears; he does not see, he partakes." [7] This delight in personality, as a literary tradition, goes back at least to Chaucer. Early novels often used their protagonists' names as titles (*Moll Flanders, Pamela, Tom Jones, Gil Blas*), and sixteen of Walpole's novels do the same.

Next to character he values "a good story": a well-constructed plot zestfully presented that leaves the reader wondering what next. His other rules for the novel are that it eschew *one-sided* propaganda (circumstances led him to ignore this axiom toward the end of his own career); that its style be unselfconscious, not "arty"; and that its tone be sincere. On sexual issues, he defends freedom of speech (though seldom using it himself).

Didactic considerations sometimes influenced his literary judgment. Joy, he responded to; despair, he could sympathize with; bored fatuity, he could not support. "This I believe to be an all-important element in a novelist's art," he insisted; "he *must* . . . feel that life, whether beautiful or disgusting, rewarding or punishing, is finally more important than himself." [8] The "selfish hedonism" of much new fiction in the 1920's undercut, for him, its artistic value. He admired its "poetry," but deplored its "soullessness"; praised its technical skill but blamed its egotism. Of noted practicers, he formed certain fixed ideas: Virginia Woolf was a poet, not a novelist; Huxley was a coldblooded scientist; Lawrence, outside of *Sons and Lovers,* was a sensual tractarian; Joyce was clever but loveless; Dorothy Richardson's stream-of-consciousness was the easy way out, and so on. Walpole was not alone in his skepticism; for traditionalists on both sides of the Atlantic—J. B. Priestley, Ellen Glasgow, G. K. Chesterton, and Somerset Maugham—made similar comments about their precocious contemporaries.

In 1925, while Walpole was writing *Wintersmoon,* he was invited to Cambridge to deliver the annual Rede Lecture on literature—a signal honor. The occasion was a great success, and publication of the lecture two months later brought good reviews. Yet today to read *The English Novel: Some Notes on Its Evolution* is disappointing. His speaking time was limited, naturally, and his subject huge, as the subtitle shows. If the content seems sketchy, it is probably because modern scholarship prefers depth to breadth; and, if the tone seems pontifical, it may be because a successful speech never sounds the same in print. The last pages concern the modern novel:

If the fading away of all the other psychology for the new intelligence of psycho-analysis and the rest is to us, as I think it is, a social gain, it brings with it for the novelist a great danger, the danger that it no longer seems worth while in life to believe in anything . . . the true work of art must come from conviction and the conviction of negation is not enough.

. . . It is not enough for [the novelist] to note the tiny earthly changes from day to day that go on around him, not enough for him to analyse the marks and scratches made by events upon his own tiny personality. Having created he must place his creations in a world that is larger than his mortal eye can scan and that has more meaning in its truth and in its beauty than his mortal brain can grasp.

Seven years later the opposition—the Hogarth Press run by Virginia and Leonard Woolf—commissioned from Walpole *A Letter to a Modern Novelist* (1932). Addressed to a fictive "Richard," who has written a novel, *Camel with Four Humps* (imaginatively reconstructed by Walpole), and wants his opinion, *Letter* is fun to read and a good sample of Walpole's views as he cites Anthony Trollope in contrast to hapless young moderns like Richard.

It would be erroneous to regard Walpole as entirely against "modern" writers. "One trait of Sir Hugh Walpole of which, I hope, posterity will not be left in ignorance, was a capacity to appreciate and admire generously the work of authors very different from himself," wrote T. S. Eliot after Walpole's death. "That he was quick to appreciate the work of younger men, and ready to help and testify to his belief in their future, is equally certain. These qualities, combined with his personal charm and unassuming manners, have, I feel sure, given him the affection of many writers with whom the public may not suppose him to have been associated." [9] This assessment is no exaggeration; but numerically speaking, of every five words Walpole wrote about the New Fiction, only two seem really favorable.

His most popular critical treatise, published the year before *Wintersmoon* and reprinted often, is *Reading*. Its three parts, "Reading for Fun," "Reading for Education," and "Reading for Love," represent childhood, adolescence, and adulthood, with Walpole's own reading experiences as examples. The first two parts are addressed to parents and teachers. "Reading for Fun" concerns, after children's "first books," historical novels, like those of Scott (discussed at length), Ouida, G. P. R. James, and the American Marion Crawford; and Gothics, like *Frankenstein* and *Jane Eyre*. "Reading for Education" covers the teen and college years: poetry (Keats, Browning, and Landor), Hazlitt's essays, Poe's stories, Lamb's letters, Elizabethan drama, *Beowulf*, George Meredith's novels (discussed at length), Walter Pater's esthetics, Thomas Carlyle's histories. "Reading for Love" discusses book collecting, and the reader is encouraged in his role as "personal critic." Walpole, listing his own favorites, boosts the Victorians; but "the field is so much larger than it was, and every man may choose to his own liking."

Endemic to *Reading* is its ingenuousness. Walpole bends over backward to make the reader feel at home and comfortable with books. Knuckle-raps such as this one are few and light: "One has often read of learned judges, Cabinet Ministers and philosophers who, exhausted with the brain-work of the day, care only for the reading of detective stories. There is nothing wrong about detective stories save that there are not, alas! enough good ones, but I have never understood why a volume of Hazlitt's Essays or Lamb's Letters or Mr. De La Mare's poetry should not be as easy

reading for these weary giants as the works of Mr. Oppen-
heim. . . ."

Jibes are not aimed at the immediate reader, for Walpole is his
ally. The author sees his reader as "the Man in the Street plus
a little culture," the "Unsophisticated reader" for whom "almost
nothing is done" by the "more superior literary journals of our
time." He himself hastens to join the ranks: "It would be flatter-
ing to my intelligence were I able to make this Essay a learned
and analytical description of any reader's proper mental processes,"
the first sentence reads. But he is too "fuzzy-minded" to do so.
Simply, he wants the reader to explore the "ecstasy" of reading
with him—and woe betide the critic, the intellectual, who inter-
feres ("one of the principal characteristics of the Sophisticated is
that they have been all at one time or another literary snobs")!

The author's disarming analysis of reading tastes includes his
own, by implication, as well as his reader's: "What one has truly
learnt perhaps, if honesty is the only wear, is that one will never
for the rest of one's days become a Reader of the finest class,
never one of those splendid persons who are orderly, systematic
and philosophical, and never one, I suspect, with that fine im-
peccable taste that can sift at once the chaff from the wheat or
perform an instant judicial separation between the sheep and the
goats."

This light banter takes a sharper edge toward the end, where
he discusses current literature (italics, mine, identify the "enemy"):

. . . an amazing number of men and women have learnt how to write
a novel that, technically at least, would have been thirty years ago
a masterpiece. . . . The result of this is that *the more literary critics . . .*
who ought to be having by reason of their great gifts real influence
over the Plain Man who is interested in literature, have none at all,
because he—the Plain Man—discovers that they are forever recom-
mending to him *Cranks and Queer Ones* whom he fails to understand.
There is at the present time a superstition far too general among *clever
people* that if a book has any large sale it cannot be good literature. . . .

Walpole's anti-intellectualism is obvious here as he lumps together
all those he considers "highbrow" or pretentious, whether writers,
critics, or "superior" readers. This attitude colors many of his
novels too, if we stop to realize it. David Blackwood Paul,
in a lecture given in Wellington, New Zealand, in 1952, notes the

"reckless body-blows at the intelligentsia Mr. Walpole was flashing round," adding, "Walpole seems to have given strength and respectability to an anti-highbrow movement." Mr. Paul suggests reasons for Walpole's attitude: vindictiveness—"When he did not get the praise he wanted [he] hit back at the intellectual characters in his novels,"—and basic incomprehension—"Walpole did not understand intellectuals." [10] Both suggestions, I think, are correct. Walpole's romans à clef testify to the first; the second we see, for instance, in his favorite hero type.

That Walpole had a favorite type of hero he agreed. "All novelists have a particular kind of hero—Tolstoi's was lean and tall, Balzac's elegant and debonair, Fielding's strong and coarse and so on. Why this is so the psychologists will explain if you ask them." Walpole's favorite type was nearest Fielding's: "short, thick set, immensely strong in the back," the hair usually wayward, the nose snubbed—"not a beauty by any means, but there was great distinction in [the] firm chin." [11] Jeremy, Peter Westcott, Harry Trojan, James Maradick, Jerry Lawrence, young "Bullock" Delaney, Archie Traill, Hans Frost—all illustrate his favorite physique. Never good at athletics, Walpole admired those who were. His favorite spectator sports besides cricket were boxing and wrestling, and they were engaged in by the kind of men he admired. In 1941, shortly before he died, he described Maradick, at seventy, as "full of life and vigour. His hair was snow white. He was as broad and strongly made as ever. No bent shoulders or ricketty legs."

Without attempting a case history, we may note that Walpole himself had most of these characteristics (the wayward hair soon thinned itself out). One of his features he did not give his heroes: eyeglasses—a significant omission. Plainly in creating his favorite type Walpole was ruling out any suggestion of a weak body or a hypersensitive mind. The latter, he felt, had been his own undoing; and, in saving his heroes from it ("I gave you the character I like best in the world—normal, solid, loyal, sensible," he tells Maradick),[12] he saved them from other things that had made the author himself "different"—that, in fact, helped to make him an author. Not all Walpole heroes are the same type, of course. But the thin, gangly ones, like Henry Trenchard (who wears a pince-nez in *The Young Enchanted*) and Cornelius, are in the minority.

Walpole does not deserve all the blame for his anti-intellectualism. Distrust of the intellect is as rampant traditionally in England as in America; and his immediate family were not intellectual in any real sense. Hugh's was the traditional Walpole strain, as his cousin Lady Dorothy Nevill (*née* Walpole) once described it: ". . . with something of the child's dislike of order and restraint, we have also the . . . child's buoyancy of disposition. . . . Erratic, . . . [our] chief characteristic, perhaps, [is] an intense love of frivolity combined with a real liking for literature and art. For music, however, few of us have cared at all, whilst most have positively hated its more serious side." [13] To this description Hugh Walpole's early pattern runs surprisingly close. Gradually, he came to like music (German opera paved the way); and slowly, much more slowly, he dropped his defensiveness in print against "culture," or the arts, as a matter for intellectual speculation. The change, which becomes apparent in the late 1930's, is given its strongest boost in his posthumous novel *The Blind Man's House.*

VIII   The Blind Man's House

In *The Blind Man's House,* Julius Cromwell, the blind man, fits Walpole's favorite physical type: strong, broad-shouldered, virile. "I believe you have twice as much magnetism in your body as people who can see," his wife, Celia, tells him. At the same time he loves the "arts"—relies, in fact, strongly upon them. Poetry and especially music are the mainstay of his existence; in place of paintings, he asks for word pictures—and gets them from his family and friends—of his surroundings. Any belief that responsiveness to the arts is somehow "feminine" is denied by the fact that his wife, fashionable young Celia, hates good music and good books, and resents their influence over him. Her conscience tells her at one point: "You might have learned at least one language properly, read some books that taught you something. You might have tried to learn what music was really about; you were too idle and self-willed to bother."

By making Cromwell wholly blind, Walpole bypasses the necessity of his wearing eyeglasses and thus seeming "weak." But Cromwell's blindness is not merely for that purpose; it is an important symbol in the topical *Blind Man's House* (1941). The frequent allusions to current events recall Walpole's "Parables of the Time" (see Chapter 4); but, unlike the mood of these novels, the mood here is affirmative—Julius Cromwell, unlike Captain Nicholas, Colonel Fawcus, Bessie Field, and James Tunstall, is no dictator to be feared and hated. We may consider Julius Caesar and Oliver Cromwell as dictators, but we think of them as "good" dictators; thus "Julius Cromwell" suggests a thoughtful, dedicated statesman.

In this role, his blindness is an asset. Walpole's thesis—that because they are spiritually attuned to their surroundings, blind people are superior: feel more, understand more, "see" more than those who depend on their physical eyes—is a familiar one. Julius Cromwell represents the clear thinking needed now when, as he puts it, "War leans on the edge of the world." The story takes place between the summer of 1938 and the spring of 1939, in a small seaside town where the wealthy Cromwells have settled recently. Already Britain is haunted by the fear of enemy planes, of which the local seagulls are symbols: "Flurries of seagulls haunted the village with screams and cries. . . . Especially did the village green appear the right place to them, for they rose and fell, rose and fell above it. Then, strutting on the grass, their red beaks lifted, they seemed to carry the village in their cold scaly eye and place it on the edge of the sea. . . . [They] moved, raising at a moment their blood-stained beaks to heaven, deliberately—arrogant owners of this lovely world."

To the residents of the small, fear-ridden town, Julius Cromwell becomes, gradually, a shining light. The local Anglican preacher, lazy, bitter, worldly, cannot help them. Still Cromwell, no saint and no celibate, is a full-blooded man; and, before he can gain others' confidence, he has his own problems to solve: a lurking thief; prying neighbors (including the preacher's wife); discontented servants; and especially his wife, spoiled, pretty, and on the brink of an affair with the good-looking Socialist gardener. Julius is not always told of these problems; but he senses them, ponders, contemplates, memorizes Milton, writes in his journal (an unreal device in his case?), listens to music, until at last he "sees" through, or around, the problems; and becomes an inspiration and example for all. This stress on the so-called highbrow arts as important aids to solving human problems is first found in Walpole's novels, as I said before (there are several glimpses in his short stories), in *The Blind Man's House*. Had he lived long enough, his fiction might have outgrown entirely its anti-highbrow tone.

The biggest concern in the full-bodied (some might call it "padded") *Blind Man's House* is Celia—for two reasons: her creator, a bachelor, was now in his late fifties; and for the last decade he had been portraying young matrons against historical backgrounds (in the Herries novels; see Chapter 7), where their role was naturally less free. (The one exception is Christina Field in the contemporary *Sea Tower*, a real "heroine" with few flaws.) Celia causes Julius a great deal of pain; and, in accounting for her doing so, Walpole describes her much as he had Rosalind Grandison in the late 1920's. Julius is speaking: "She's been brought up anyhow. No religion, no codes. There's no reason for her why she shouldn't do anything at all that she wants to. Any kind of spiritual world seems to her nonsense. She's got the creed of her post-war generation that there *is* no creed, that life's a cheating business with no purpose, and the only thing to do is to get as much out of it as you can. At least that *would* be her code if she were not so kindly, sweet-hearted, childlike."

Thus wealthy young Celia Cromwell, so vital to her husband's mental well-being in 1939—a decade after Wall Street and on the brink of World War II—is portrayed as a mixture of Lady Brett in Hemingway's *The Sun Also Rises*, Daisy in Fitzgerald's *The Great Gatsby*, and Rosalind in *Wintersmoon*: all from ten years before her time, when the type apparently fixed itself in Walpole's mind. More than any of his other novels, *The Blind Man's House* is crippled by Walpole's misunderstanding of the modern female mystique.

CHAPTER 7

Romanticist

AFTER the very successful *Wintersmoon,* which criticized Bloomsbury, Walpole, paradoxically, attempted a Bloomsbury novel himself, *Hans Frost* (see Chapter 3)—"writing, I fear, rather in V. Woolf's manner. . . . I like this book. It's in a new vein for me," he told his diary (June 1, 7, 1927). "Virginia Woolf has perhaps liberated me. . . . How can I help it when she is such a darling. . . ?" Mrs. Woolf remained the only Bloomsbury writer he really liked, but *Hans Frost* was not the success *Wintersmoon* had been. A wholly new tack seemed advisable; and for it Walpole turned to a favorite genre of his juvenilia days: the historical romance. To revive this form, neglected since the demise of Robert Louis Stevenson, Marion Crawford *et al.,* would be a real contribution, Walpole felt, to the literary scene; and the result was his famous Herries series.

Years later, in an undated note to Rupert Hart-Davis, editor Thomas Mark described his publishers' first reaction: "The arrival of the manuscript of *Rogue Herries* caused some consternation at the office. Sir Frederick [Macmillan] said to me, 'Just look what Hugh Walpole has brought in!—an enormous historical novel— and he said he's going to write three more about the same family.' We all felt doubtful about the prospects of any historical novels in those days and thought that H. W. had gone far out of his proper field. But when I read the proofs I felt that we had nothing to worry about."

Indeed, they had not; for the success of *Rogue Herries* (1930) led to Hervey Allen's famous "rogue" novel, *Anthony Adverse,* and to a multitude of historical fictions—including Margaret Mitchell's *Gone with the Wind* and Kathleen Winsor's *Forever Amber,* a female-rogue tale—which flooded the market in the 1930's. Some have called these books "escape fiction" designed to soften the blows of the Great Depression. In the long run perhaps this was true; but

Rogue Herries was composed before the Crash (Dec., 1927–Jan., 1929). For Walpole, the novel meant "escape" in another way—from the claims of traditional Realistic fiction, whose apogee he had reached in *Wintersmoon,* and from the demands of the New Fiction, which he could not or would not fulfill. The Depression and World War II helped, but otherwise is it too much to say that the Romantic *Rogue Herries* single-handedly turned the tide against the "intellectual" fiction of the 1920's (which remained unimitated, except in France, for almost thirty years)?

Like much historical fiction, the Herries novels are regional, thereby allowing Walpole to salute the part of England he loved best, Cumberland in the Lake Country. "In literature the regional has always a chance of immortality," he wrote; "for if the author can make the reader feel that there is in this square of ground that he is describing a beauty unique and eternal, his writing will be kept alive as a guiding hand to that beauty." [1] He had visited the Lake Country in his teens when his father was a visiting preacher in Cumberland. During five summers they clambered, bicycled, sketched, and stared at spots he would know and admire a hundred times after returning to live there permanently (he retained his London apartment) in 1924. The last chapter of *Wintersmoon* occurs in Cumberland; and *Farthing Hall,* which Walpole (between *Hans Frost* and *Rogue Herries*) wrote with J. B. Priestley, divides its setting between the Oxford-London area and Cumberland.

I Farthing Hall

Farthing Hall (1929) takes place in modern-day Britain, although its delightful epigraph reads like a scene from an eighteenth-century farce:

FAGG
Sir, there has been a great spattering of ink
among these gentlemen.

PURDEN
Doubtless they have known great affairs.

FAGG
Nay sir, 'tis all fantastick, I'll swear; so
many silly toys and fables, out-moded fripperies,
worse than your Grub Street gear.

PURDEN

Well, for my part, Master Fagg, I'll take an oath
that truth casts a shadow or two here as she
does elsewhere.

Act IV. Knighton's
*Devil Take the
Hindmost* [2]

In plot and structure also the novel owes much to the eighteenth
century; a "Northanger Abbey phantasy," Mark French, one of the
characters, calls it. Like Jane Austen's famous novel, it parodies
the eighteenth-century genre founded by Horace Walpole: the
Gothic romance. Young French, a painter, plays it straight as the
impressionable Romanticist whose flights are tempered by his
Realistic friend and correspondent, Oxford professor Bob Newlands. As French at one point writes to him: "You have reduced
by your mere presence the whole Rossett family to more ordinary
terms—Jean is a pretty girl with dark eyes, the elder Rossett a
good old country squire, Farthing Hall itself an ordinary little
country house. I can see that in your own mind you have found
me absurdly unreal with my whole view of that romantic scene,
it isn't romantic to you at all."

The novel is composed of the two men's letters and telegrams
—an echo again of the eighteenth-century vogue of epistolary
fiction. American publishers Doubleday, Doran offered a prize
to the first three readers guessing which letters were written by
which author.[3] Priestley was ten years younger than Walpole and,
of their *personas,* Newlands is forty, French twenty-six; but anyone knowing Walpole's work would identify him with French,
who becomes involved in rescuing a young woman from her
formidable guardian. This familiar plot, used first in *Maradick
at Forty* and repeated in *The Young Enchanted* and in *Portrait
of a Man with Red Hair,* Walpole was to use again in *Rogue
Herries* and *The Joyful Delaneys.* In all but *Farthing Hall,* the
guardian is unfit, even dangerous; in two (*Man with Red Hair*
and *Rogue Herries*), the rescue actually requires his death. But
in *Farthing Hall* under Newlands' mild scrutiny, French's romantic escapade ends in a triple marriage, including that of the
strong-willed squire to a female religious fanatic. Since the religious fanatic has almost wrecked Newlands' marriage by per-

suading Mrs. Newlands to leave her husband for a more exalted career, the squire's wedding benefits the professor too. The story ends with everyone "happy and in love."

Watching two authors handle the same characters—the autocratic father; the pretty daughter; Mr. Trump, the inn owner; Mrs. Newlands; and so forth—is instructive. Priestley, himself from the North, reproduces the Cumbrian dialect which Walpole avoids (although he used it later in the Herries books). But, while the novel sold surprisingly well,[4] *Farthing Hall* is not meant to be taken seriously. A spoof, a lark—let us leave it at that.

II Rogue Herries

After the joint labor, however whimsical, of writing *Farthing Hall*, Walpole returned thankfully to composing by himself. And, in so doing, he produced his masterpiece—*Rogue Herries;* in my opinion Hugh Walpole's best work. *Judith Paris*, the second Herries, though less well done, is good (among his "bests" I would put it sixth). The third Herries novel, *The Fortress* (1932), in both style and structure is one of the worst books he ever wrote; and *Vanessa* (1933) is ordinary. Together, the four novels cover two centuries: 1730 to 1932. For *Bright Pavilions* (1940), the fifth, written after a lapse of years, Walpole dipped back to Elizabethan times. It is better than *Vanessa:* more spirited and more compelling. He had planned another tetralogy, but *Katherine Christian* (1944), successor to *The Bright Pavilions,* was unfinished because of his death. Between the unfinished *Katherine Christian* and *Rogue Herries* lies a gap of 127 years (1603–1730).

It would be a mistake to think of the Herries books as mere costume classics. While writing each of them, Walpole immersed himself in the history of its era. Twenty-five broadsides, tracts, and volumes, for instance, on a single event in *Rogue Herries*— the Jacobite Rebellion on behalf of "Bonnie Prince Charlie"— were in Walpole's library when he died.[5]

The novels, replete with local color, emphasize topography. Heretofore most readers were familiar with the Lake District through the works of the immortal Lake Poets, Samuel Taylor Coleridge, Robert Southey, Thomas Gray, and William Wordsworth. Between these nineteenth-century celebrants and Walpole, L. C. Hartley makes this distinction: "If one is steeped in descriptive poetry of the Lake District written prior to 1850, one may feel that the beauty of the region is entirely idyllic. . . . To Mr. Walpole the vision is a more virile and dynamic one. This is not merely a land of placid lakes and green hills and pastoral calm; but it is also one of bareness and scars and restless energy." [6] Western mountains; rolling sheep fields and meadows marked by long walls of white stones; startling, dramatic lakes—Walpole paints them all.

Could the Herries stories have happened anywhere else? It's hard to say. All sometimes divert to other locales. Judith Paris goes as far away as France. *Bright Pavilions* and *Katherine Christian* begin in the South of England. Rogue Herries—moody, temperamental, restless—could have appeared in any part of England as an outlander, been equally unhappy there, and launched an equally prolific breed. Cornwall or "Glebeshire" might have harbored such a man and made no more change in him and no less than the Lake Country does. But Walpole considered such regions too quaint and confining for a figure of Herries' tragic stature.[7]

Herries' given name is Francis. His Cumberland neighbors, however, disappointed that the newcomer is not rich, and outraged by his brazen mistress, elaborate oaths, and wild gallops across country, dub him "Rogue"—rascal and madman. Later, he sells his mistress at a fair; and, after his long-suffering wife dies, he falls in love with redhaired Mirabell Starr, thirty years younger than himself. Reared in a smuggler's cave, she is an elusive young creature when they first meet. Time passes, and her sweetheart is killed in the Jacobite Rebellion. Reluctantly, she marries Francis, but soon abandons him. A thrall to unscrupulous lovers, she stays away for years.

Francis, adoring her, has mellowed. Now, waiting for her, he humbly takes up farming; and "Rogue" becomes an affectionate neighborhood nickname. The change marks a new stage in his fortunes, suggesting the novel's theme: "Be patient and selfless and you will be loved." His wife, aged by misuse and deprivation, at last returns. They are happy and decide to have a child, but Mirabell does not live through the birth. Francis, extremely ill also, dies in the next room at the same moment.

Despite the strength of the final scenes and Mirabell's spiritual importance to her husband's well-being, she is only the tritagonist. We see a great deal more of David Herries, Francis' son by his first wife. We observe the father first through the son's eyes when the family, traveling northward to its new home, stops over-night at an inn. David shares the bedroom with his sisters and his father's mistress (their nursemaid)—and, for a short while, with his father. The boy comprehends nothing as he watches the actions of this man he so admires; and the room's atmosphere is a medley of dark walls, flickering firelight, and pending adventure overlaid by drowsy innocence. "As long as I live, I shall remember the first scene of 'Rogue Herries,'" said Gerald Gould. "This is the pure stuff of romance, never old, never worn, never tarnished." L. A. G. Strong twenty-five years later still thought it "one of the loveliest and most memorable scenes in the literature of our time." [8] Another fine chapter is "The Sea—Father and Son," in which David, now eighteen yet treated as a child by Francis, asserts his manhood. Its psychology—the covetous felineness of the father, the masculine doggedness of the son—is admirable. In two chapters, called "The Saga of David: I" and "II," he acts alone, minus his father as foil. This section is the weak spot of the book as Walpole deploys again the melodramatic plot line of *Farthing Hall* and others: a young girl's escape, aided by her lover, from a wicked guardian.

Outside this episode David is matter-of-fact and rather simple, in contrast to his complex, mood-torn father. This version of the "doubles" pattern occurs frequently in the Herries novels: two figures closely related by blood, but one is solid and practical, the other, emotional and inconstant. Rogue Herries, as Marjorie Bowen says, "is as delicately self-tortured, as morbidly self-conscious (and as fluent in saying so) as any product of modern intellectualism." Yet Gerald Gould makes an astute judgment: "What I cannot quite get *at* . . . is the central spring of personality, the impulse that drives [Herries] on through such violent diversity." [9] No inherited genes and no nihilistic education account for his misery and wildness in the first half of the book. As a younger son, he is victimized by the English law of primogeniture; but this factor is not stressed. Aside from this ambiguity and the weak "Saga" chapters, *Rogue Herries* is very good indeed.

One of its finest features is its rhetoric, Walpole's traditional style, now at its greatest. Surer even than in *Wintersmoon,* his prose has more sweep, more verve, and an attractive spontaneous irony. Another asset is the author's new willingness to drop the old conventions in depicting sexual relationships. Finally, its many vivid, dramatic scenes—Francis' confrontations with his older brother Pomfret, the drowning of a local witch, and so forth—make it exciting to read, almost wearing, in fact.

"Hundreds a week," Macmillan's told Walpole (Diary, March 10, 1931), were being sold in Britain a whole year after publication; particularly popular in the Lake Country was the expensive, keepsake leather edition. In the United States *Rogue Herries* was one of two Walpole titles (*Wintersmoon* was the other) to reach *annual* best-sellerdom. A prairie newspaper exulted that the *Rogue* was "no milk for babes—but meat for strong men—good old English roast beef, hung till it is 'high,' and eaten rare." [10]

III Judith Paris

The brash vigor of *Rogue Herries* is lacking in *Judith Paris* (1931). With so open, so unabashed, an antihero as Francis Herries, the *Rogue* had pained many of the Walpole faithful. "The letters I've been getting from old ladies," he exclaimed to Harold Macmillan (July 31, 1930). Even the usually cool-headed *Times* spoke of its "lurid language." [11] While we can imagine the astonishment of, say, *Green Mirror* fans encountering *Rogue Herries* (or vice versa!), its language seems today restrained enough. The Herries books were never so "coarse" again—unfortunately, for Walpole's surrender not only muffled his new frankness but dulled the edge of his satyr-like humor.

So the old ladies who complained about the *Rogue* had less cause to quibble about *Judith Paris;* and the Julian Green house with its "old rickety staircase" down which, in *Judith Paris*, Georges Paris is hurled to his death in the small Cumberland hamlet of Watendlath, became an object of pilgrimage for admirers,[12] who apparently preferred murder to "muck". There are many turbulent scenes in the book. Near the end Judith, "sitting in the carriage, only half-awake, in this shrouded world," thinks of "her four friends, all dead from violence": Francis Herries, David's son, who has shot himself; pious Reuben Sunwood, killed defending David's old house, where Francis' immoral widow still lives; Georges, Judith's French husband, "whom she had loved and still loved," thrown downstairs and his back broken by the father of a slain seaman; and Warren Forster, Judith's lover and her child's father, dead in Paris of a heart attack during a political riot. Except for Francis' suicide, Judith is present on each occasion—as is the reader. As with *Rogue Herries*, reading its successor is emotionally exhausting. Although a man would enjoy it, *Judith Paris* is essentially a woman's book —a "women's lib" book, in fact; for Judith refuses to marry her lover, not because she still loves Georges but because "A woman gets farther by going it alone."

Three chapters are especially skillful. "Francis Rides Over" shows Judith as a vital, poised young matron with a quick wit. "The Herries Ball, May 17, 1796" reveals the characters and motives of the guests as they approach and perpetrate "the case of the broken fan," an apparently insignificant incident—a kind of "Rape of the Lock" in its trivial beginnings and far-reaching effects that reverberate through the rest of *Judith Paris* and provide the motive for *The Fortress*. In "Family Papers," ten years of Judith's life are covered by letters between several correspondents, with Walpole distinguishing nicely among them, their characteristic attitudes, concerns, and styles. (The wittiest one, Jennifer Cards, he is at pains later to present as stupid and sluggish—an odd slip in characterization.)

With no deuteragonist, *Judith Paris* is an unusual Walpole novel. Judith herself combines the two Herries strains represented in *Rogue Herries* by Francis and David, respectively: the emotional and the practical. To quote Marguerite Steen (277), Judith is "flame in a duffle gown." Some have thought her story the best of the Herries novels. J. B. Priestley, Walpole's collaborator on *Farthing Hall*, for instance, "likes 'Judith' immensely much better than 'The Rogue' and [says] she is my best heroine" (Diary, Aug. 12, 1931). The last judgment is true. Otherwise I agree with Walpole, who wrote Thomas Mark, "I never expected that *[Judith]*'d be liked so much better than 'The Rogue.' 'The Rogue's' better really you know" (September 18, 1931).

Certainly *Judith Paris* can be read with pleasure; the style in the first three quarters is only slightly less grand and moving than the *Rogue*'s. In Part IV, however, the phrasing and diction are distinctly foreign to the setting (early nineteenth century) and to the rest of the book. Walpole was starting this part when Somerset Maugham's *Cakes and Ale* came out, and his suddenly reckless tone may be laid to the hurt and resentment he felt (see below) over Maugham's portrait of "Alroy Kear," a pushing, popular author with Walpole's looks and some of his mannerisms. We can finish *Rogue Herries* and feel that the story is complete, but not *Judith Paris,* whose final chapter points like an arrow to its sequel. This would be less annoying if the sequel were good. But it is not.

IV The Fortress

Walpole promised, when Macmillan's agreed to charge higher prices for the Herries books, that they would be long.[13] This may account for the padding in *The Fortress* (1932): too many scenic descriptions and too much pageantry. Or perhaps, by writing the equivalent of a three-decker Victorian novel, he was merely aping its period (1822–74). The book begins with a long recapitulation— the only time in the series Walpole uses this device for bringing newcomers up to date. The rest of the story he tries to liven with italics and exclamation points, scenes of pie-throwing farce, a horsewhipping, and a bloody diorama of murder and suicide. But the novel remains comatose, and its style is pure fustian. Scenes between Adam Paris and his German wife, the main "love interest," are synthetic and trite.

More than any other Herries novel, *The Fortress* lacks what Henry James would call a "centre." The author leans heavily on his privileges as omniscient consciousness. Judith Paris is still at hand, but things are seen as often from others' viewpoints: her cousin Walter's, his son Uhland's, Uhland's sister Elizabeth's, Elizabeth's husband John's, Judith's son Adam's, Adam's wife Margaret's, and so on.

The Fortress itself is a huge, ice-cold Gothic manor which Walter Herries has built on a ridge overtowering David Herries' old house, now occupied by Judith. Walter intends the Fortress to symbolize his domination of the Herries family, a struggle for power begun in *Judith Paris* with the broken-fan incident. But Walter loses. If any force holds the Cumberland Herries' together, it is tolerant Judith, who lives out her second half century ("growing old by fits and starts among the fells," as one amused critic said) [14] in this very long novel. As it ends, she is celebrating her hundredth birthday with Walter, whose mind is failing, in attendance. I have covered only the main story-line, but the subsidiary plots are variations on the same theme, the stupidity of family feuds—which could be enlarged to mean the stupidity of

holding grudges against anyone—Somerset Maugham, for instance. That *The Fortress* served as a personal battleground for
Walpole did not help it as art.

V Vanessa

Vanessa (1933) merits slightly more consideration than *The
Fortress*. Compared with its betters in the series, it lacks the
exciting adventure-story plot of *The Bright Pavilions* (discussed
below) and the vivid, compelling style of *Rogue Herries* and of
most of *Judith Paris*. As the female title figure of a Herries novel,
Vanessa is far less alive than her grandmother Judith. Distressed
by the continuing acclamation of Maugham's *Cakes and Ale,* of
which Walpole saw himself the butt, he concluded that the public
preferred cynicism to wholeheartedness. In his diary he wrote of
Vanessa, "[she] promises well if I don't get too fond of her"; and
of Adam Paris, Judith's son, "He is my favourite hero since
Harmer John. I must be a little ironic and sarcastic about him
I suppose. It makes other people like him better" (Dec. 28, Apr.
8, 1931). What it did, of course, was make Adam and Vanessa less
convincing. More at ease with the boyish redhead Judith Paris and
less confident anyway when composing *Vanessa*, Walpole hardly
seems to know what to do with his heroine, a gentle dark-haired,
fair-skinned girl with vaguely religious instincts.

Vanessa is a "dreamer." In the Herries novels "dreamers," as
we know, are doubled usually with "doers"; but the contrast of
Vanessa with her cousin Rose Ormerod is founded on moral
grounds. Rose's behavior, similar in some ways, is really an inversion of Vanessa's. Soon after Vanessa's disastrous marriage,
Rose leaves her weak husband for the first of a string of lovers.
Vanessa's rise on the social scale (although she is not a "climber")
contrasts directly with Rose's successive steps downward. Later
Vanessa also sins, in the eyes of moral law; but, in her heart, she
has been faithful to her lover, Benjie, all her life. This faithfulness
and her leaving him to spend the last years of her life caring for
her deranged husband, make it possible, Walpole implies, for
her to die a saint. The terms of her sanctification comprise the
novel's theme. A few days before Vanessa's death, Rose dies too,
an outcast. She and her affairs serve as a buffer for Vanessa, whose
actions conventional readers might otherwise attack.[15] (We noted

this same guilt-deflecting scheme in *Above the Dark Circus* and in *Prelude to Adventure*.)

The most skillful scene in *Vanessa* is Mafeking Night, celebrating a great victory of the Boer War. The same event was portrayed in *The Duchess of Wrexe*, but Walpole twenty years later handles it much better. The Duchess' family crosses Vanessa's path often, and her fatal engagement to Ellis occurs in 1885 at the Duchess' ball. Thirteen years later Vanessa herself gives a ball, where she meets Rachel Beaminster and senses the impending clash between the girl and her grandmother. The following day Vanessa visits the Duchess' portrait in a scene that echoes the first chapter of *The Duchess of Wrexe*.

Part I, Vanessa's childhood and adolescence, is weak. Following the inept technique of *The Fortress*, Walpole splinters the viewpoint of the novel among Vanessa; her cousin Benjie; their illegitimate daughter, Sally; and Benjie's legitimate son, Tom. But the book's greatest weakness is the last two hundred pages: Part IV, covering the years 1912 (when Vanessa dies) to 1932, when the novel was published. The heroine now is Sally, the illegitimate daughter of Vanessa and Benjie; and the language she and her friends use, slangy and crude, is a pathetic example of Walpole's lack of ear for the speech of the postwar generation. He wrote Part IV reluctantly for, as he told Rupert Hart-Davis (333), he "saw that the Herries thing properly closed in 1914, and that the whole post-war business refuses to fit the mood and colour of the rest." But he had promised four l-o-n-g Herries novels, and that promise was kept.

VI *Hugh Walpole and Somerset Maugham*

I have referred briefly to Somerset Maugham's novel *Cakes and Ale* (1930) and indicated something of the effect it had on Walpole, who was caricatured in it. The affair devastated him, not only personally but artistically; and for that reason it deserves more than passing mention. Maugham was ten years older than Walpole, yet their careers were strangely parallel. Both attended King's School, Canterbury (Maugham in the year Walpole was born). During World War I, they were in Russia at the same time. "Delightful lunch with Willie Maugham," Walpole's diary (Oct. 20, 1917) observes. "He most amusing and decides he has got as much of Russia as there is to get. Which isn't bad as he's been here about four weeks!" (It was Walpole's third year there.)

As fictionists competing for the same public, they shared the same American publisher; and their reputations ran neck-and-neck for years, a fact that must have galled the creator of *Of Human Bondage*. Maugham's reputation is now in the lead—perhaps rightfully, but partly also because he put a spoke in Walpole's wheel at the crucial moment. Several chroniclers, including Mr. Hart-Davis, have recorded Walpole's temporary loss of face and his personal agony; [16] but none has assessed the damage done to his career artistically. Of Walpole's six best novels, in my opinion, four were written, one after the other, between 1925 and 1930, the year of *Cakes and Ale*.

The cause of this phenomenon is not completely clear. If the plural *causes* is more descriptive, we should surely include Virginia Woolf. This is no time to trace their friendship, which began in 1923 and deepened steadily (Hart-Davis, 240, 289–90); but we ignore at our peril this comment in his journal (January 14, 1929): "I don't want to be confident, and certainly not complacent, but I think Virginia has shewn me—especially in *To the Lighthouse* and *Orlando*—how to get over a little of my sententiousness and sentimentality. I think both *Hans Frost* and *Herries* show the beginning of this change. . . . Anyway God be praised for giving me so thrilling an occupation!" Clearly, he felt himself to be on the right track artistically. The subsequent arrival at his door, on September 25, 1930, of *Cakes and Ale* interrupted the winning streak of *Wintersmoon, Hans Frost,* and *Rogue Herries,* and as we have seen, swamped the last part of the otherwise-good *Judith Paris*.

Why did Maugham attack just then? He and Walpole had seemed to be good friends.[17] Was it jealousy, the outraged sensibilities of a fellow-craftsman, or some more personal matter—something Walpole had written recently, for instance, such as *Hans Frost?* Because Frost is a prominent author with an over-possessive wife, rumor had it that he was based on Thomas Hardy, recently deceased.[18] Actually Hans is rather like Robert Frost with the plot of Edith Wharton's novel *Ethan Frome* thrown lightly around his shoulders. Walpole met Robert Frost in America shortly before starting the novel; but Somerset Maugham, across the Atlantic, could hardly have known this. Maugham himself was a literary man with a wife some thought unsatisfactory. They were divorced the year *Hans Frost* was written. The book displayed, moreover, Walpole's unexpected gift for comedy; and Maugham rather fancied himself as a wit. Also there was the rumor linking Hans with Thomas Hardy. . . . So Maugham wrote *Cakes and Ale*. It was wittier than *Hans;* and the hero sounded even more like Thomas Hardy. And Maugham included for good measure a character whose "head is cut off with a golden axe on nearly every page of the novel," as one Maugham biographer has said.[19] This was Alroy Kear—who was clearly Hugh Walpole. Maugham at the time denied both likenesses; and his protestations to Walpole were perfervid.

Too hurt—and wise—to threaten libel, Walpole's self-questioning soul reacted drastically. As Hart-Davis explains (316),

> . . . Alroy Kear is a novelist and lecturer, a time-serving eupeptic careerist, a literary and social snob, determined at all costs to build himself up into a grand old man of letters. . . . All successful writers are the envy of less successful ones, and although Hugh had never deliberately wronged anyone, there must be some whom he had slighted. . . . From among such groups a likely set of enemies could speedily be conjured up. And now this cruel caricature of Maugham's had placed a dagger in their hands. No wonder he was worried.

Sensitive, insecure, and wanting desperately to believe this man he had thought was his friend, in public Walpole joked it off. "I shan't forgive Willie easily. The beggar had drunk my claret," he told drama critic James Agate. "As the horrible novelist in Maugham's new novel remarks (he bears a dreadful resemblance to myself and six at least of my friends including Maugham): 'We all do our best,'" he chattered in a magazine column.[20] Heartbreak was left for more private moments.

In 1950 when Modern Library published *Cakes and Ale*, Walpole had been dead nine years, and Maugham at last confessed the likeness. "Hugh Walpole was," he asserted, ". . . the most prominent member of that body of writers who attempt by seizing every opportunity to keep in the public eye, by getting on familiar terms with critics so that their books may be favorably reviewed, by currying favor wherever it can serve them, to attain a success which their merit scarcely deserves. . . . He was a genial creature and he had friends who, though they were apt to laugh at him, were genuinely attached to him. He was easy to like, but difficult to respect." [21]

Putting aside the question of whether Maugham's judgment is overharsh (I think it is, although it is easy to see how it came about), we return to our first query: What was the effect of all this on Walpole as an artist? Exactly how much damage was done? In the late 1920's, he was riding high, deservedly so: his writing had more richness and zest than it had ever had for so long a period. When *Cakes and Ale* appeared, Walpole's style in the last part of *Judith Paris* fell away immediately from the gracious, fluent prose of the rest of the novel. Anachronisms sprang up as modern slang, usually violent, escaped the characters' lips. "You are damn right about the tempo and colour changing in the last quarter," Walpole wrote fellow-author Francis Brett Young, not bothering to explain.[22]

Above the Dark Circus, serialized earlier in the *Evening Standard,* was being published as a book. Walpole seldom changed his work once it appeared in print; but on re-reading *Circus,* he found this passage near the end, spoken by Dick Gunn: "Osmund was right. Life might do its damnedest and I would be on the side of the Affirmers—I was on the side of Life whatever personal catastrophe involved my little private history." Walpole ripped out this passage. It was painfully appropriate, and it sounded like the complacent, platitudinous Alroy Kear. The tale is stronger for this and other terminal changes he made at the same time. Nevertheless, *Above the Dark Circus* and *Judith Paris,* published the same year, were Walpole's last good works for nearly a decade.

During the next three years Walpole wrote his two worst novels, to my mind: *The Fortress* and *Captain Nicholas.* The first was doomed from the start when we recall the conditions under which he had finished *Judith Paris;* for, after *Cakes and Ale,* his will to succeed slumped badly. The scrapbook, now at the University of Texas, in which for years he kept personal clippings and other items of interest, stops abruptly at the date when Maugham's novel appeared. As though revived by adrenalin, it resumes the following March with reviews of *Gin and Bitters* by "A. Riposte." [23] *Gin and Bitters* was an acrid attack on Maugham, "a novel about a novelist who writes about other novelists," as its jacket reported. It was soon discovered that a woman writer,

Elinor Mordaunt, was hiding behind "A. Riposte." Whether her grudge against Maugham was fostered by pity for Hugh Walpole ("Mr. Polehue" in the novel) or by reverence for Thomas Hardy is unclear. Although her novel gained a hearing in the United States, *Gin and Bitters* was withdrawn in England (where it was titled *The Full Circle*) after selling only a handful of copies.

Walpole had a part in its withdrawal, to the amusement of some onlookers who considered his behavior a quaint kind of cowardice. When the chuckles reached him, he issued a statement through the *Daily Mail:* [24] "I am not out to defend Somerset Maugham, and I thoroughly resent the suggestion of myself as a noble person turning the other cheek in public. . . . I was not a prime mover in the persuasion of the author to withdraw *The Full Circle* or a defender of Somerset Maugham. He is well able to defend himself. But many of us thought the book so nauseating that if such works were allowed to become general, they would do harm to English letters and something like horsewhipping would have to be revived. . . ."—an exaggerated image revealing Walpole's continuing agitation. In his book column, meanwhile, he continued reviewing Maugham's works justly and without rancor.

The year 1935 witnessed another cry from his heart about the Maugham affair. In the preface of *Mr. Perrin and Mr. Traill*, reissued by Everyman's, he apologized for the liberties he had taken, twenty-four years before, with real people and real events at Epsom College:

. . . Mr. Somerset Maugham, who has frequently been accused of putting into his books people who are directly taken from life, . . . has said, what is absolutely true, that it is quite impossible for an artist to put down on paper (if he has any creative power at all) a portrait of someone he knows—the portrait will change in his hand. Quite so; but the real trouble lies in the surviving fragments of the actual person. . . . *Moi qui parle*—I have suffered and I know, and I frankly consider that there has been in my time a great deal too much of this. It is inartistic, often very cruel, and always unnecessary.[25]

A cry from the heart? Certainly—but a hypocritical one; for at that moment Walpole was engaged in the practice he was excoriating yet could not resist: in *John Cornelius* the many à clef figures include Maugham as "Archie Bertrand" and Walpole

[130]

himself as "Simeon Rose." Both are authors. After analyzing Rose objectively and at length, the narrator says of Bertrand: "He is both in his outward self and in his books, a cynic, a pessimist, and above all (what he most wishes to be) a realist, a man who sees things exactly as they are. . . . But within, Bertrand is, I think, self-assured, rather arrogant and deeply sentimental. He is, in fact, the man whom Rose tries to be in his writings, while Bertrand's writings have the cynicism that is in reality deeply embedded in Rose's character." Although Rose and Bertrand are minor figures, they are an interesting version of the inverted-doubles pattern.

Some reviewers of *Cornelius,* expecting a return to the bluntness of *Perrin,* were disappointed. V. S. Pritchett complained that "handling [Cornelius] as if he were a piece of old Staffordshire makes him tedious. One turns to the pictures of literary life hoping to find a few scores paid off, but it is all done with warm handshakes and forgiveness . . . all cakes and no ale," he concluded slyly.[26]

VII The Bright Pavilions

Enough has been said here about the Maugham-Walpole story to support my case that Walpole's writings were consistently poorer after September 25, 1930, when he "picked up idly Maugham's *Cakes and Ale.* Read on with increasing horror. Unmistakable portrait of myself. Never slept" (Diary). Of his novels after *Judith Paris,* none (*John Cornelius, The Fortress, Vanessa, The Inquisitor, Captain Nicholas, A Prayer for My Son, The Joyful Delaneys, The Sea Tower*) offered much hope that he was rallying as an artist until *The Bright Pavilions* (1940). Even then, the impulse behind his fifth Herries novel was more religious than artistic. Its background is the Elizabeth I–Mary Stuart quarrel; its main weakness is the lingering, derivative [27] account of Mary's last days that occasionally retards the action.

In taking Mary's side against Elizabeth, and thus against Protestantism, Walpole echoed family history. Four Walpoles of "ultramontane zeal" were reconverted to Catholicism in Elizabethan times; one, Henry, like Robin Herries of *The Bright Pavilions,* was martyred in 1595 for becoming a Jesuit.[28] As the son of an Episcopal churchman, Walpole had been critical of Catholicism; but a trip to Rome in 1939 to report the coronation of Pius XII for the Hearst papers confirmed his growing interest

in that direction, and he returned home to finish two books concurrently: *The Bright Pavilions* and a moving account of his
journey, *Roman Fountain* (see Chapter 8).

Bright Pavilions is better-than-average Walpole, not because of
the historical setting—we get rather tired of Mary Queen of
Scots—but because the religious theme is conveyed through a
good adventure story. The love interest is slight; aside from the
two queens, the female characters are poorly drawn—"duds,"
Walpole called them. "Was there ever an Elizabethan woman in
a novel worth tuppence?" he asked himself (Journal, Oct. 18,
1939).

Mostly the novel is a tale of derring-do; unremitting pursuit,
temporary escape, and finally fierce retribution. "At about midday
Nicholas Herries threw Philip Irvine over the fell down to the
Valley. Felt a great elation as I wrote this," Walpole's diary observes (the same date). Irvine is a villain from Elizabeth's court
responsible for Robin's apprehension and torture. The title phrase
"The Bright Pavilions" (taken from a poem by William Blake)
is used often during the book by Robin to describe what he hopes
heaven will be like. He dies on the torture rack: "The screw
turned again, but now he felt no pain, for he was away, away,
and the Bright Pavilions were in sight at last, standing in the
sun-white sky." The contrast between the brothers is the usual
one in a Herries novel: Robin is the dreamer; Nicholas, the doer.
That the protagonist is Nicholas does not mean that doing is
better than dreaming—for this would have meant disowning a
later dreamer, Rogue Herries, Nicholas' great-grandson.

Both Francis the Rogue and Robin "see" the white horse—a
symbol linking *The Bright Pavilions* with the rest of the Herries
books. Robin Herries is asleep:

Immediately in front of him was a deep black tarn, bounded by an
ice-sloped hill, and in the tarn struggled a magnificent white horse.
He watched, longing to help, unable to move. The great horse, with a
tossing white mane, fought to escape from the tarn. Its hooves struck
the ice but could not hold; with a great heave, as it seemed in his
dream, of all the strength there was in the world, it struck and struck
again, almost fell back, but caught firmer hold and was up and away,
white against white, lost in the snow.

An important symbol throughout the Herries books, the white horse represents an abstract ideal. Marguerite Steen (262) describes it as "the vision of all the seekers of that Beauty [that is] beyond Beauty." The vision shows itself only to the most sensitive of the Herries', i.e., most sensitive to mental influences. At times actually perceived with the eyes, at other times it is imaginary, part of a dream or an image sketched suddenly on the mind. In the mind of crazy Uhland (in *The Fortress*) the vision is twisted: he sees a black horse. In the same novel, young Jane (child "seers" are frequent) draws a white horse on a piece of paper and gives it to her uncle, John Herries. John has seen the white horse too from time to time. Now on his way to fight Uhland, he takes the drawing with him. After killing John, Uhland writes his own suicide note on the back of Jane's sketch, indicating his literal reversal of the ideal.

Carl Jung (who admired *Prelude to Adventure*—see Chapter 5) has translated "horse" as "intuitive understanding"; and a horse emerging from water, frequent in the Herries novels as in Robin's dream, is said to "symbolize the cosmic forces that surge" from "primigenial chaos." [29] The color white means life. Thus, seeing the white horse marks the seer as someone special though not necessarily the protagonist. Some minor family figure, like Jane in *The Fortress*, may be vouchsafed the vision. Whoever receives it, the vision comes, as it does to Robin, as a sign of grace.

Popular response to *Bright Pavilions*, the last of Walpole's novels to be published before his death, was good. Twenty-eight thousand copies were sold in the first three months (Hart-Davis, 438), and American critics liked it. Some British ones were less sure. Markedly favorable was the theology-oriented *London Quarterly Review*, to whose reviewer the novel "demonstrated [that] he was approaching the height of his power." Writing after Walpole's death, the reviewer added: "It looked as though he might be on the threshold of the promised land of great achievement for which his distinctive, if at times wayward, pilgrimage had seemed to be preparing him." [30]

I cannot go this far. Whether Walpole's new vigor, traceable seemingly to religious inspiration and evident in *The Bright Pavilions*, would ever have produced works as fine as those he had written ten years before, when his impulse was artistic, seems doubtful. Thus I repeat my conviction that *Cakes and Ale* had more to answer for than anyone up to now may have realized—except Walpole himself.

VIII Katherine Christian

After finishing *Bright Pavilions,* Walpole made retreat in Dorset with a group of Anglican monks; and five months later he repeated the visit. The seed of faith sown in his youth by his church surroundings, whether he liked them or not, had become assimilated and was growing deep roots. *Katherine Christian* (1944), the last Herries novel, centered again on religion, the struggle between the Cavaliers and Puritans. Although the story was unfinished when Walpole died on Whit Sunday, 1941, it comes to a kind of conclusion with the burning of Mallory, old Nicholas Herries' Sussex home, during the Civil War. The fact that his son Robert has been knighted by Charles I for financial help to the Crown has put Nicholas in the Puritans' bad graces.

Although the book as a whole cannot be recommended, the scene of the Roundheads entering Mallory is well done; and there are good portraits of James I, Charles and Cromwell—*"most* original," Walpole wrote to Thomas Mark (Jan. 19, 1941): "all warts and buttocks." The plot is built around two brothers of opposing faiths: Rashleigh, a Cavalier; and Peter, a Roundhead (as in *Bright Pavilions,* where Nicholas was a Protestant, Robin, a fledgling Catholic). Rashleigh and Peter are not Herries, but their grandfather was, and they are second cousins of Nicholas and the martyred Robin.

Nor is Katherine Christian a Herries. Her father is a magician, a traveling conjurer; and the significance of his surname, "Christian," is a matter for conjecture. Katherine—a more believable heroine than any in *Bright Pavilions*—as a "Christian" is a Mary Magdalene. Originally a little wild girl, like Mirabell Starr in *Rogue Herries,* she becomes a statuesque adventuress with a fine soul in a corrupt body. Influenced by the wholesome love of Peter, the Puritan, she reforms just before the book ends: an appropriate close to the work of a writer who was becoming more deeply interested in the spiritual side of things.

One other coincidence may be mentioned. Written two weeks before his death, a chapter in *Katherine Christian* recounts the betrayal of the Earl of Strafford—material that Walpole forty years before had used to write his juvenilia novel "Strafford." As Rupert Hart-Davis (442) justly observes, "The circle was completed."

CHAPTER 8

Other Fiction, Other Prose

I *The Short Stories*

HUGH WALPOLE is most respected for his novels, and rightly so. His short-story collections—*The Silver Thorn* (1928), *All Souls' Night* (1933), *Head in Green Bronze* (1938), and *Mr. Huffam* (posthumous, 1948) [1]—received, on the whole, good reviews; but most of the stories are mediocre. Walpole's temperament contributed to his lack of success in this genre, for he knew the "rules." With his uncritical expansiveness, it was hard for him to concentrate on a single character in a single important episode for a single effect. "No one who is essentially a novelist is also a sanctified short-story writer," he remarked in the Cumberland Preface to *All Souls' Night;* "and the moment's experience . . . comes to me very seldom detached" (ix). To him, short stories were money makers and nothing else.

Moreover, he could not use the same models for his stories that he used for his novels. Nineteenth-century British traditionalists had not excelled in the theory and practice of short stories as a conscious art form. Thus he and others of his era looked abroad to certain acknowledged masterpieces. From America, they had the atmospheric tales of Poe and Hawthorne, practiced with deliberate art; the "slick" surprise-ending stories of O. Henry; and the sentimental Western tales of Bret Harte. From France, they had Flaubert's and De Maupassant's careful studies of the lower and middle classes; and, from Russia, Chekhov's deceptively simple sketches of private lives. Some of Walpole's contemporaries—Katherine Mansfield, D. H. Lawrence, and James Joyce—later became models themselves by adapting the French and Russian methods to their own.

At one time or another Walpole imitated each of these types successfully, but the proportion of his successes to his failures is small. His stories as a rule sound like undigested lumps from novels. A setting lovingly dwelt on, a character sketched at length—then suddenly he seems to recall, "I'm writing a short story!"; a deus ex machina, a new person or a new personality trait, is introduced; and the close comes quickly. Other stories "trail off at the end like wounded soldiers," his diary admits (Mar. 3, 1926). Both methods reveal a lack of control. Yet, except for juvenilia, only a few stories in manuscript in the Walpole files at the University of Texas remain unpublished. From the start of his career, he had little difficulty selling whatever he put on the market on either side of the Atlantic. His short stories, despite their weaknesses and his lack of interest in them, not only sold immediately but were included in other editors' anthologies. The dog stories and terror tales were in special demand.

Other than juvenilia, Walpole wrote about 105 short stories, three dozen of which I think really good; of these, a third are superior. For what may be called a "cream-of-Walpole" collection, I would choose twelve. Each follows roughly one of the four conventions described above: (a) the Poe-Hawthorne tale of portentous atmosphere, (b) the slick O. Henry story with its witty surprise ending, (c) the Flaubert–De Maupassant Realistic study of character, (d) the more subjective Chekhov-Mansfield character sketch.

There are overlappings; but of the atmosphere stories I recommend Walpole's "The Tiger," which metamorphoses New York City, its heat and its traffic, into a lurking maneater. "Red Amber," a presketch for *The Old Ladies* set in Polchester in the 1890's, is another gripping atmospheric tale. The O. Henry category, witty and commercial, is represented well by Walpole's "The Exile," in which a bit actor in Hollywood, homesick for England, can't tear himself away in an actual showdown; and by "Green Tie," a "most embarrassing moment" short-short with a piquant close. Stories with carefully detailed study of character would include "The Oldest Talland," the skillful picture of a well-meaning summer visitor in conflict with the fiercely primitive Tallands in a tiny Cornwall port; "The Enemy," in which a self-convinced victim gladly continues his subordinate role after the victimizer dies (a foretaste of *The Killer and the Slain*); "The Brother," a gentle tale of two refined old-maid sisters who allow their beloved, much-traveled brother to defraud them; and "Bachelors," a well-plotted story of two brothers pathetically but humorously divided by a picture and a girl.

Finally, of the impressionistic Chekhov-Mansfield stories, I recommend "The Dove," a slow-starting but nightmarish portrayal of a traveling Englishman victimized by Germans after World War I; "The Critic," a satirical short-short about a professional critic who dreams one night of being a novelist; "Turnip-Lanterns," in which a trio of youngsters welcome home admiringly a supercilious schoolboy; and "The Monkaster Feast," written when the author was fifteen, a blunt, ironic description of an evening's "fun" planned for children that fails.

The last two stories are still in manuscript; three of the others are uncollected.[2] My criteria for this list are vigor of style, consistency of plot (feasible cause and effect) built around a provocative situation, and "timelessness" ("Absalom Jay" and "Half-Way Upstairs" would be included if they were less topical). Some of Walpole's stories repeat characters from his novels. In "Half-Way Upstairs" and in "The Dog and the Dragon" the protagonists are Beaminsters (the Duchess of Wrexe's family). In "The Oldest Talland" the summer visitor is Mrs. Comber, from *Perrin and Traill*. Peter Westcott narrates "The Honey-Box" after the death of Millie Trenchard, whom he married in *Young Enchanted*. "Church in the Snow," "Carnation for an Old Man," and "The Silver Mask"[3] deal with further Herries. And eight-year-old Jeremy returns in "The Ruby Glass."

II *"Fragments of Autobiography"*

If the English literary tradition could not help Walpole write short stories, it provided excellent models in autobiography, popular in Britain since 1800. As an author, he appreciated the fact that memoir writing was an art without fixed "rules." In fact, his memoirs display qualities that would have made his short stories more successful: apt touches of characterization, atmosphere that does not overweigh the action, the exact climactic phrase, the precise final word. These traits are, of course, those of a good *raconteur*—"and as a talker Hugh was at his best in descriptive reminiscence," Rupert Hart-Davis tells us (290). He avoided writing a full-fledged autobiography, protesting in *Roman Fountain* (1940), "This isn't an autobiography. No, no. It will be twenty years before I write one." If *Roman Fountain* is "not autobiography," what is it?—a little fiction perhaps,[4] something of a travel book; but in length at least, it is Walpole's most ambitious autobiographical effort. Briefer and earlier are *The Crystal Box: Fragments of Autobiography* (1924) and *The Apple Trees: Four Reminiscences* (1932).[5]

The Crystal Box has eight chapters. After "Childhood," which centers on his school experiences (cf. *Fortitude*),[6] "Cathedral Piece" describes the author in his Durham years—a gawky adolescent with overweening pride grinding out juvenilia and imbibing the atmosphere of a bustling English town dominated by its cathedral. His remarks about Durham Cathedral ("it appeared to me to have become pagan and heretic through its history of blood and crime") and the people connected with it ("Everybody disliked someone; everyone was intriguing against someone else") recall *The Inquisitor* and of course *The Cathedral*.

Chapter III, "Ships and Souls," describes his year as missionary on the Liverpool waterfront—one of the "greatest failures of my life":

In a ship especially I was out of place and ill at ease. I was not sincere enough in my religion to forget myself. . . . I found that I was beginning to have an affection for the heavy drinkers. . . . My adjurations faltered; I was found one afternoon drinking beer with the cook of a certain steamer and laughing immensely at his not very seemly jokes. I liked the cook, I liked his jokes, and because he was a good fellow with an admirable sense of humor I was forgetting altogether his need of heaven. . . . The Mission to Seamen was, and is, a splendid institution . . . but it needs men of a certain type to carry it through and I was not of that type.[7]

"London, 1909–1914" describes the established authors, especially Henry James and H. G. Wells, who befriended the young writer newly arrived in the city. "Russia" discusses Walpole's duties in Petrograd; "Glebeshire," his writing of *The Cathedral*; "Books—and Then Books," his reading since childhood (cf. *Reading*). "And Now—" is a defense of the traditional novel; and, with the dictum "In art there is no progress but only a procession of interpreters," *The Crystal Box* closes. Supposedly the box itself, an object of beauty and purity lost but not forgotten, is a legend passed on by an ancient aunt to the author as a small boy.

Because *The Crystal Box* was privately printed, one hundred fifty copies only, it is rare; fortunately, though, it was also serialized. Not so *The Apple Trees*, of which five hundred were printed; and they are extremely elusive. Some critics have preferred *The Apple Trees* to many of Walpole's novels. "The style of this little masterpiece is exactly eleven and a half times better than its author has ever achieved before," proclaimed one.[8] The title is from Virginia Woolf's novel *The Waves*, as quoted by Walpole in the first chapter (ellipses are mine): "The apple-tree leaves became fixed in the sky; the moon glared. I was unable to lift my foot up the stair. . . . I shall call this stricture, this rigidity 'death among the apple-trees' for ever . . . we are doomed all of us by the immitigable apple tree." This metaphor reminds Walpole of a piece of ground, half "entangled garden," half stunted orchard, attached to the family's Durham residence; and we get a fuller account of those unhappy years. Chapters Two and Three, "Prelude to Adventure" and "Henry James's High Hat," deal with pre-World War I London: his early financial straits, his first job at a literary agency run by Americans, his passion for the stage, publication of *The Wooden Horse*, and sketches of certain literary figures, including Thomas Hardy, Arnold Bennett, and supremely Henry James. The last chapter, "Sower Myre Farm," deals again with boyhood memories when, during summers away from the hated Durham, he stayed at a Cumberland farm. Its tangled garden had no apple trees, only pleasant associations; and the book ends as, "the owl hooting in the tree at the end of the garden . . . while the moon stroked the floor," he falls asleep.

In Walpole's last autobiography, *Roman Fountain* (1940), the fountain conventionally symbolizes creativity and immortality. The symbol is especially appropriate for this account of his trip to the Eternal City to report for the Hearst papers the burial of Pius XI and the crowning of his successor. Walpole, as his diaries show, was strongly critical of the church ("Holy? I didn't wish them to be holy," he admits in *Roman Fountain*); but the new Pope Pius XII impressed him. The fountain that he claims to have seen as a young man on his first trip to Rome, and to have since sought vainly, symbolizes man's hidden but vital soul to which, he feels, the election of the new Pope will bring fresh hope. Ingenuously enthusiastic, *Roman Fountain* should be read by those interested in the occasion it commemorates or in Hugh Walpole himself.

A brisk, day-by-day account of his mission (based on his diary

[140]

and the articles for Hearst) is supplemented by passages of reverie. We have sketches of his parents, descriptions again of his unhappy school days, accounts of his previous trips to Rome, vignettes of author-friends, and references to things he has written. He discusses his personal quirks frankly and, in a less confessional vein, his tastes in painting, sculpture, poetry, church music, historic ruins, and modern dictators. The longest chapter describes his five "ideal" Renaissance figures: Pope Julius II, Niccolo de' Niccoli, Girolamo Ogliati, Aldo Manuzio, and Michelangelo. When Harold Macmillan wanted to cut what he called the "learned chapter," Walpole demurred (October 20, 1939): "Readers like a little bit of solidity in the middle of a book like this. . . . I would like the whole book to be about . . . the Renaissance!" *Roman Fountain* is easier to obtain than *The Crystal Box* and *The Apple Trees*, but the advantage of reading all three is obvious. While certain topics reappear, they are treated differently each time. Facts sometimes go awry in the process, but attitudes change as the author himself grows in experience and, seemingly, in wisdom.

III   *Recurrent Motifs in Walpole*

Mention of the fountain symbol recalls various motifs discoverable in Walpole's works, although Walpole need not be studied at length as a conscious symbolist. While alive to the effectiveness, even the inevitability, of symbols, he seldom employs them in a deliberate pattern. The main exception is the white horse (see Chapter 7), a motif that runs through all the Herries books. However, we should note a few others that, conscious or not, seem just as obvious. Such a survey is also another legitimate way of organizing the large corpus of his work.

While most Walpole motifs are traditional, their complexion is his—the very fact that he chose some and rejected others reflects his personality. A few have already been discussed in relation to specific titles: fountains (*Roman Fountain;* important also in the lives of two spiritual pilgrims, John Cornelius and Harmer John); strangers (*Captain Nicholas* and others—see Chapter 4); blindness (*The Blind Man's House;* important also in other works of his last decade, *Katherine Christian, The Inquisitor*, and the short story "Service for the Blind"). The forest motif in its frustration, battle, and sexual aspects is found in *The Dark Forest*, also

[141]

in *Portrait of a Man with Red Hair, Maradick at Forty,* and the short story "A Field with Five Trees."

Every Walpole motif is either beneficent or maleficent, either "good" or "bad." Blindness, fountains, the white horse, and (usually) strangers are beneficent; forests are maleficent. *Authority figures*—whether animate or inanimate—are maleficent. Youth dramatizes the objects it rebels against, and the aftermath of his own youthful rebellion stayed with Walpole through his career. *Grandparents,* like old Mr. Westcott in *Fortitude,* Sir Jeremy Trojan in *The Wooden Horse,* and the Duchess of Wrexe are authority figures to be denounced—an attitude related to the archetypal urge of man-as-animal to kill the old leader and become the new. Even less enviable is the role of *fathers.* In Walpole's fiction, conflict between father and offspring is nearly always oedipal—between father and son, not father and daughter; if the latter exists potentially, as in *The Captives,* the daughter sublimates it in Victorian fashion.

Whether family figures or not, men with beards, especially *white beards,* fill a malevolent spot in the author's pantheon. Since beards in his day were unfashionable, men wearing them were considered Victorian throwbacks, a link with authoritarianism that lent them a grim air. Moreover, God was pictured with a beard; and so were Old Father Time and Death itself, as in Chaucer's "Pardoner's Tale." Such beards were white, so it is not surprising that Walpole's white-bearded men are awesome individuals—nor that white beards, far from representing the traditional purity of their color, mean hypocrisy and double-dealing. We recall Jeremy's anguish (see Chapter 5) at the fickleness of Jehovah; and Jehovah's pagan stand-in, Jupiter, usually pictured with a white beard, is notoriously capricious. No matter how saintly in appearance, how gracious in manner, Walpole's white-bearded men make mischief. The heartless headmaster in *Perrin,* Moy-Thompson, is the first of a long line of authoritarian white-beards who do as much harm as they can.

Female authority figures also are objects of suspicion. Implacable, self-centered, domineering, Walpole's *mothers* follow a type of English literature discussed by Clemence Dane in regard to *The Green Mirror.* Mrs. Trenchard, Miss Dane notes, represents "custom, law, the immovable object. . . . The strong-

minded woman has always had a special place in English literature. . . . Not for nothing is England represented as a lady in
a helmet with a trident, and sitting down. That conception of
her must have arisen through an unacknowledged but general
realization of the characteristics of the typical Englishwoman.
. . . The novelists, from the beginning of the novel, have observed
and used this female tragedy," Miss Dane adds, ". . . and seldom
with sympathy." She cites Scott, George Eliot, Jane Austen, and
Anthony Trollope.[9] Walpole, who sees maternal possessiveness
as mixed love and self-aggrandizement, depicts aggressive mothers in *Fortitude, The Young Enchanted, Wintersmoon, Hans
Frost,* and *The Fortress;* and he reaches horrendous heights with
his portrayal of Bessie Field in *The Sea Tower.*

Towers themselves are inanimate authority figures because of
their shape and height; and, because they point toward heaven,
imagination has seen them as agents of a deity either beneficent
or maleficent. Suggesting captivity, their presence accents the
thralldom of one or more characters in the novel. Towers are
important to the landscape in *Maradick at Forty, Portrait of a
Man with Red Hair,* the werewolf short story "Tarnhelm," *John
Cornelius* (near the school John teaches at briefly and hates), and
of course in *The Sea Tower.* Towers are also a phallic symbol,
and readers interested in psychoanalysis should be able to explain
their presence as such in *Maradick, Red Hair,* "Tarnhelm," and
The Sea Tower, if not *Cornelius.*

Another inanimate authority, the *clock,* is personalized by
Walpole. Clocks fascinated him; and, of the scores mentioned in
his fiction, each is described with care. Most are grandfather
clocks with odd faces. They have distinctive ticks—"coughs,"
"wheezes," "hiccups"; their pendulums are like long beards on
old men; and they watch people and are inimical to them. The
following description is representative: "The great grandfather's
clock, with the gold heads of Chinamen on it, muttered 'Come-
here, come-here, come-here!' [Billy] wouldn't come, because the
clock might do something very horrid to him if he did." Here,
by chance in a children's story,[10] are the grandfather element, the
odd esthetic detail, the speaking ticktock, and the sense of horror and impending punishment. Early in his career (1913) Walpole wrote "The Clocks," a story of a slow-witted youth who

kills his grandfather and is afterward driven crazy by the clocks in the house. The old man's name is "Tackity"—an unmistakable presentation of clocks as authority figures.

But, as the list at the start of this section shows, not all Walpole motifs have to do with authority. We have mentioned the Herries' white horse. Felines and canines too have their place. Archetypally, members of the *cat* family represent a hidden, unpredictable force. Hitler, Mussolini, and Stalin in Walpole's journal (Jan. 7, 1939) are "the Tiger Dictators." In *The Duchess of Wrexe,* "tiger" is used frequently by Dr. Christopher, the Beaminster family doctor, to mean the *id,* the seat of man's subconscious amoral instincts; and the good doctor urges various characters to acknowledge the "tiger's" presence, "tame" it, and make constructive use of its energy. In the short story "The Tiger," the beast is portrayed more literally as the underside of civilization. The roar and stink of New York City become those of a great tiger caged beneath the streets—hot-breathed, ruthless, ready to leap and destroy the unready; and there is no talk of "taming." *Housecats* too are dangerous. Two, in fact, malicious Becky Sharp in *Captain Nicholas* and possessive Penelope in the story "The White Cat," are killers. Black Becky, sly Nicholas' "familiar," his double in feline form, literally frightens sick old Mrs. Carlisle to death; and Penelope brings death to her mistress' avaricious suitor. Becky assaults poor Mrs. Carlisle in the flesh, while we are led to believe that Penelope appears in the spirit to her unfortunate victim.

Dogs in Walpole are, on the other hand, a beneficent motif; and critics frequently remarked about his skill in portraying them. "One wonders who [else]," commented the London *Times* in 1938, "among writers to-day, understands them so well." [11] He does not personalize dogs by giving them human speech ("Poodle" in *Jeremy and Hamlet* is the sole exception) or by making them walk on their hind legs. His attitude toward his canine characters is as careful and attentive as toward human ones, sometimes more so. To reverse the usual conceit, if there were a way for a human being to become a canine (I am not speaking of werewolves), Walpole must have known it—he seems to get inside their skins. His dogs are not like people, they *are* like dogs; and the reader is sure of it!

Space permitting, other motifs might be discussed: such as

uncles (beneficent), aunts (maleficent), fights and carnivals (maleficent), and schools (ambivalent). But we conclude with the word "*rose*," whose role in Walpole is an unusual one: not the flower *per se*, but as the proper name of places and people he clearly admires and as an adjective referring to his favorite portion of the color spectrum. Three-year-old Angelina in *The Golden Scarecrow* calls her new doll Rose: "Rose had been kept, as a name, until some one worthy should arrive." Seemingly, this statement expresses the author's own attitude. In *Hans Frost*, portraying his close friend Virginia Woolf, he calls her Jane Rose; and depictions of Walpole himself in the later novels bear the name Simeon Rose. The highest ideals of international friendship are represented in *Prayer for My Son* by Rose Clennell, who works in the League of Nations.

His approbation of the word "rose" extends to the entire red spectrum. Is it mere coincidence that Nicholas' quick-witted fiancée in *Bright Pavilions* is named "Rosamund," while in *Golden Scarecrow* there's an autobiographical nine-year-old called "John Scarlett"? That Garth in *Roselands* is the village Katherine Trenchard loves—the village where, thirty-five years later, Julius Cromwell (in *Blind Man's House*) surmounts his personal problems? That Christina Field in *Sea Tower* works *her* problems out in a town called "Scarlatt"? That the girl Mark French chases halfway across England is surnamed Rossett? That an idolized piece of red amber precipitates the plot of *The Old Ladies?* That a ruby vase is the object most highly prized by Jeremy's family? That the surname of Walpole's favorite woman character (Diary, July 8, 1918; Journal, Sept. 30, 1924), Maggie in *The Captives*, is Cardinal before she marries?

Overbalancing the horrid "man with red hair" are several admirable redhaired figures in the novels: vivid Judith Paris, Walpole's best-drawn heroine; Mirabell, Rogue Herries' beloved; Judith's son, Adam Paris, a favorite of the author; Clare Westcott *(Fortitude)* and Maude Penethen *(Harmer John)*, unpleasant perhaps but sparkling and intense; and gay little Rupert Herries, the liveliest figure in the incomplete *Katherine Christian*. In Walpole's personal life, it seems significant that the destruction of the "Pink Terraces" in New Zealand (so called because of the lovely color of their volcanic soil) when he was three remained with Walpole as his first esthetic memory.[12] Interviewers often commented on his love of red clothes—particularly cherished were successive pairs of "cherry-coloured" trousers (Hart-Davis, 442); and his favorite flower was the red carnation. Knowing his personality, we can see his love for rose and red as a support for the side of him that was determinedly optimistic. Many people wear "rose-colored glasses," but few carry the literal color into what they write as much as Walpole did. If still in doubt about its importance, we can remember Dick Gunn's talisman in *Above the Dark Circus:* a rose-colored *Don Quixote* with "a crimson leather label." Rose and red constitute Walpole's good-luck motif, a weapon against the maleficent dark.

CHAPTER 9

Review and Perspective

I A Review

THE literary prestige of Hugh Walpole, once high with the reading public and with the critics on both sides of the Atlantic, collapsed almost completely after his death. Confronted with this phenomenon, we naturally ask ourselves: why was his work esteemed while he lived, why did its reputation fade, and is it likely to revive? Our study of his writings and of the literary era spanned by his lifetime, suggests some answers.

Among the many traditional writers of his generation Hugh Walpole was the most prolific and (partly through his lecture tours) the widest known. His energy, sincerity, and volubility, although they gained him enemies, resulted in a personality cult that ended necessarily with his death. In 1914, we recall, Henry James had included Walpole in his approbatory essay "The Younger Generation" in the *Times Literary Supplement*. Besides many kind words in private,[1] Joseph Conrad became publicly involved in Walpole's career to the extent of writing a preface for the *Hugh Walpole Anthology* (1921). The very fact that there *was* such an anthology was of course a commendation.[2]

For a time, Walpole's work was given serious attention by flourishing critics like Arnold Bennett, by the more contemporary W. L. George [3] and Joseph Hergesheimer, and by younger writer-critics like J. B. Priestley, Joseph Warren Beach, Clemence Dane, Marguerite Steen, and L. A. G. Strong. His works, especially his novels, were appreciated for their traditionalism in a period when the New Fiction of authors like Virginia Woolf and James Joyce was failing to satisfy most readers and certain critics, educated in the "grand old tradition" of Fielding, Dickens, George Eliot, the Brontës, and scores of others.

But time passed, and Walpole lost credit with several of the main critics, especially as the New Fictionists themselves began to fill that role. In retrospect, it seemed obvious that James's prophecy of success had been a mere expression of faith. The Conrad preface too was not glowing—although its prim dryness was as Conradian as James's sifting and resifting was typical of him. Arnold Bennett, after doing his duty by Walpole as he emerged, through Bennett's publisher George Doran, onto the American market, preserved for the most part a public silence about his friend's fiction. Women critics Rebecca West, Katherine Mansfield, and, later, Elizabeth Bowen had few kind words for him; and John Middleton Murry followed Miss Mansfield's lead. Among the younger critics, L. A. G. Strong remained his most discerning supporter. From Strong's scattered writings about Walpole (see the Bibliography) what emerges is a clear, convincing portrait of the man and his work still far from all-out approval. What was there in Walpole's writing to cause reviewers, as their attitudes toward him slowly crystallized, to be dissatisfied? "My aim, if I have any," he stated once in a brief autobiographical note, "is to write novels that will follow the main tradition of the English novel, but that will be aware of the modern technique and modern psychology." [4] The validity of these goals allowed, why did critical acclaim of his work lag gradually behind popular acceptance?

Were contemporary critics determined simply to propagate the avant-garde novel of Virginia Woolf, James Joyce, Gertrude Stein et al.? Obviously not. Joyce, for example, has never been especially admired by the English literati; as for American innovators, what attention was William Faulkner receiving in those years? It was not so much that Hugh Walpole followed tradition but that he failed to attain its highest standards. Most modern traditional critics, Susan Sontag notes, believe that if the novel "has a serious purpose (something other than mere diversion, entertainment, escape) it is this: the responsible and intelligent dramatizing of psychological and social and ethical issues, and the supplying of information." [5] On the other hand, Walpole's approach to writing was largely an emotional one.

No author ever believed more fervently in variety; for, to him, each book was a fresh, new venture. If it failed him, or if he failed it, along the way, this failure was regrettable and could be laid to such faults as carelessness and egocentrism, as he was well aware. The point is, he did little to change them! Perhaps he could not. Besides, when one is rich and well known through exercising the trade he loves, why should he try radically to change?

Walpole became increasingly involved, meanwhile, with lecturing, chairing of the Book Society, and writing scripts in Hollywood; and Hollywood and lecturing meant months at a time out of England, where he did his best writing. Yet he seemed happiest when busiest. At the same time he was a fatalist; and optimism and fatalism alternate in his diaries and journals, as here (Journal, Jan. 4, 1928): ". . . I do not see why on occasion one should not count one's blessings and render thanks. It does not mean that I have self-pride . . . or have achieved anything. I am conscious of extra ordinary [sic] luck. All kinds of disasters may be (and probably are) in store for me." Two years later, the unfortunate Maugham incident occurred (see Chapter 7), slashing directly across the added burst of energy released in Walpole when he became friends with Virginia Woolf and her circle, whose work he admired and, in his own way, tried to emulate. If to Maugham's exploitation of him as "Alroy Kear," we add Walpole's wavering health during the final decade of his life, we see why his best books were all written by 1931.

II *A Perspective*

Possibly his most calculated piece of work was his first published novel, *The Wooden Horse.* So serious was he about it that he sent it to three established writers, as we know (see Chapter 2) —Charles Marriott, Ethel Mayne, and E. M. Forster—for help, gladly using their suggestions. Actually his dependence on helpers in one phase or another of his writing never ceased. We find Sir Edward Marsh—statesman, patron of the arts, and connoisseur-about-town—shepherding Walpole through *Perrin, The Duchess of Wrexe,* and *The Young Enchanted*—even reading galley proofs. When Walpole was called back to Russia the galleys of *The Green Mirror* were left to a fellow novelist, J. D. Beresford, with disastrous results. And when, despite Marsh's help on *The Young Enchanted,* several embarrassing errors slipped by, Macmillan appointed a special editor for Walpole. In a history of the firm by Lovat Dickson, Thomas Mark's aid is overstated: Walpole never left proofreading entirely to Mark, as Mr. Dickson claims; but he did rely on him heavily. "You have absolutely saved my reputation by guarding so wonderfully [against] my inaccuracies!"

he wrote Mark on one occasion. "Others have their uses but you are the one and only who knows whether the moon rose East or West Jan: 3 1630." And to Harold Macmillan he described Mark as "my guiding star, my Socrates, my suckling mother." [6] Certainly their relationship, which existed for the last twenty years of Walpole's life, contributed to his inborn carelessness and effervescence.

Other faults, most of which I discussed in previous chapters, are discernible in his fiction—his overuse of the journal-diary-personal letter device; his avidly self-conscious depictions of physical brutality; his attribution of personal traits unsupported by speech and action; his inexplicable vacillations in style; and his reliance for emphasis on "very" and, at the other extreme, his phrases like "I think," indicating a tendency to hedge. Ends of novels are hard to write, but Walpole usually finished his in a burst of speed. And every book he wrote is at least sometimes sentimental.

The virtues of his lesser works (even *Captain Nicholas*, the worst, has some) are outnumbered by their defects—those just mentioned and others: clichés of situation and of language, episodes retold several times, through explication, dialogue, and, say, the protagonist's diary; motives recapitulated in the same way; and self-analysis placed in the mouths of characters incapable of understanding, let alone expressing, themselves. In Walpole's best novels, however, these defects must bow to positive advantages such as overwhelming sincerity, compelling style, genuine humor, and characters that are alive.

There are two echelons of what I call "Hugh Walpole bests"— works transcending the irresponsibility and obtuseness that he may indulge in elsewhere. Supreme, in my opinion, are the historical romance *Rogue Herries*, the ecclesiastical exposé *The Cathedral*, and the Russian novel *The Dark Forest*. Only slightly less good are the next three—all, with *Rogue Herries*, from the vital late 1920's: the urban homily *Wintersmoon*, the light-hearted artist-tale *Hans Frost*, and *Rogue Herries'* successor, *Judith Paris*. Nor would I limit Walpole's readability to these six novels. Besides the memoirs and short stories discussed in Chapter 8, nine of the minor novels seem to me well done and timeless enough to appeal to present-day readers. Like the top six, all should be kept in print. Three are bizarres: *The Gods and Mr. Perrin* (the

American version of *Mr. Perrin and Mr. Traill*, which has never
been out of print), *Above the Dark Circus*, and *The Old Ladies*.
The others are more traditional: *The Secret City*, *The Captives*,
Fortitude (the abridged version), *The Bright Pavilions*, *Jeremy
and Hamlet* (for youngsters), and, period piece though it is, *The
Young Enchanted* for its tour de force. Readers may question my
choices. The Herries books especially, through the years, have
been a target for opposing camps, one considering them Walpole's
apex; the other, his nadir. Some think his bizarres the only Walpole novels worth remembering; others are unaware that he even
wrote bizarres.

Hugh Walpole's death in 1941 was overshadowed by the events
of World War II; and by war's end much of his work, even to the
lay reader, seemed "prewar" in mood as well as in date. (He
shared this fate, of course, with other traditionalists of his generation, as well as earlier ones like Bennett and Galsworthy.) His psychology was not deep enough for the polemicist, his diction not
free enough for the returnee, and his zest was distasteful to a
public weary of personal commitment. Since 1960, I need hardly
add, this atmosphere has changed.

Among younger readers today there is an interest in the sensational, even morbid, act of Romantic introspection which finds an
echo in many Walpole works—a theme in them which J. B.
Priestley feels has been "surprisingly ignored." [7] Older readers
fond of the traditional novel need, perhaps, to be reminded that
Hugh Walpole wrote traditional prose with moral awareness,
gusto, and diversity. Many good writers today still practice the
traditional novel. Dozens might be mentioned, including C. P.
Snow, Pamela Hansford Johnson, Anthony Powell, and Graham
Greene in England; James Purdy, Bernard Malamud, and Elizabeth Spencer in America. Contemporary mores permit their works
a less inhibited content than Walpole's although he, like them,
does depict mental weakness, homosexuality, and fierce and sud-
dent death. Solidity in character handling is another feature of
their novels. As in Walpole, the author tells us about his characters; sometimes as first-person narrators, the characters "tell"
about themselves. But the revelation is controlled; there is little
if any stream-of-consciousness, for instance. Nor are readers left
in doubt as to what the characters as people, or their clothes,

houses, streets, towns, and the landscapes that surround them "look like."

These authors value diction and syntax as a means of clear expression; complex language is thought a drawback. "Structure" follows established models, and the emphasis is on plot, as it is in Walpole's fiction. Like his, most of their novels are designed to be read at a leisurely pace, although hopefully not a languid one. Sincerity marks the authors' tone—sincerity toward their stories, their readers, and their art.

These comments are generalizations, of course, but maybe I have said enough to show that Walpole's literary world is closer to our own than many in recent years have realized. Obviously, Hugh Walpole is not a forgotten genius; yet there is no reason why his work, or parts of it, should not be revived—and soon. In the likeness of his *then* to our *now*, he has much to offer us.

Notes and References

Chapter One

1. James Agate, *Ego 2* (London, 1937), p. 37. Walpole played the Vicar of Blunderstone in the MGM production.

2. The usual list includes Walpole, Francis Brett Young, Gilbert Cannan, J. D. Beresford, W. L. George, Frank Swinnerton, Compton Mackenzie, J. B. Priestley, Oliver Onions, Rose Macaulay, Sheila Kaye-Smith, Viola Meynell. (See Frank Swinnerton, *Swinnerton, An Autobiography* [New York, 1936], pp. 280–81.)

3. March 19, Apr. 2, 1914, pp. 133–34, 157–58; rptd. (rev.) as "The New Novel," Henry James, *Notes on Novelists* (New York, 1914), pp. 314–61.

4. Virginia Woolf, *Mr. Bennett and Mrs. Brown* (London, 1928), pp. 4, 17, 18; rptd. in *The Captain's Death Bed,* Leonard Woolf, ed. (New York, 1950), pp. 94–119.

5. Virginia Woolf, "Modern Fiction," *The Common Reader* (1925; New York, 1953), pp. 151, 153.

6. Rupert Hart-Davis, *Hugh Walpole, A Biography* (New York, 1952), p. 290; hereafter cited in the text and these notes as "Hart-Davis." Mrs. Woolf's only known review of a Walpole novel, *The Green Mirror* (in *Times Literary Supplement,* Jan. 24, 1918, p. 43), is unsigned, of course.

7. The Fiction Room, Toledo (Ohio) Public Library, in spring, 1971, had six Walpole titles on the open shelves and thirty-two in storage.

8. *Joseph Conrad, Anthony Trollope, Reading: An Essay, The Cathedral, Farthing Hall, Fortitude,* and *Jeremy.* (Philip J. McNiff, ed., *Catalogue of the Lamont Library* [Cambridge, Mass, 1953], *passim.*)

9. See note 5, Chapter 6.

10. In Hollywood: *David Copperfield,* "Kim," *Vanessa* (from his novel), *Little Lord Fauntleroy*; in England: *Jamaica Inn, And So—Victoria.* "Kim" was not used. (Gavin Lambert, "Shadow Upon

Shadow: Hugh Walpole in Hollywood," *Sight and Sound,* XXIII [Oct.-Dec., 1953], 78–82.)

11. Frank Luther Mott, *Golden Multitudes* (New York, 1947), pp. 286-87.

12. T. F. Maddrell to G. H. S. Walpole, Oct. 22, 1893, on file at the University of Texas (hereafter cited as "UTex."). Hugh Walpole, Diary, June 22, 1919; hereafter his diaries and journals are usually cited in the text.

Chapter Two

1. See Bibliography for complete list.

2. See *The Apple Trees,* p. 72.

3. "The Book," 1901–2, was a later, similar production (on file UTex. under "Notebooks. Bede College"), as was the "Christmas Miscellany," [1901, 1902].

4. "The White Rabbit" was his school nickname. (See "Prologue, Hugh Seymour" in *The Golden Scarecrow.*)

5. A frequent mistake in reference books, that *The Wooden Horse* was written while Walpole was at Cambridge, seems to have originated with Arnold Bennett. (See note 13, below.)

6. Of the original ten to twelve chapters, six remain. Part of III, all of IV, and two fragments listed as "Unidentified Novels" are on file at UTex.; I, II, and the rest of III are at King's School, Canterbury.

7. Anon., *Athenaeum* (June 12, 1909), p. 697. Anon., *Observer,* June 6, 1909, p. 5.

8. "Cumberland Preface," wherever it occurs in the text, refers to the special prefaces Walpole wrote for the Cumberland Edition of his novels. (See Bibliography.) Walpole and Rudolf Besier were co-authors of a play, *Robin's Father,* based on *The Wooden Horse* and produced in Liverpool in 1918 with fair success. (Hart-Davis, p. 177.)

9. Henry James to Walpole, May 13, 1910, quoted in Hart-Davis, p. 77.

10. Anon., *Spectator,* CIV (June 4, 1910), 934–36. Anon., *Times Literary Supplement,* Apr. 28, 1910, p. 174. Diary, June 10, 1910.

11. This is the single analogy between *Maradick* and *The Tempest* discussed by Marguerite Steen, *Hugh Walpole* (London, 1933), p. 99; hereafter cited in the text as "Steen."

12. Preface, *Mr. Perrin and Mr. Traill,* Everyman ed. (London, 1935), p. xiii. A film based on the novel and produced by Arthur Rank in 1948 updated the action to post-World War II.

13. Arnold Bennett, "Hugh Walpole, A Familiar Sketch," *Book News Monthly,* XXXII (Apr. 1914), [371].

14. "Why I Wrote the Jeremy Stories," *John Bull,* March 26, 1932, p. 20.

15. Cyril Connolly, "Mr. Perrin or Mr. Traill?" London *Sunday Times,* March 20, 1955, p. 5.

16. Henry James to Walpole, Apr. 15, 1911; when Walpole protested, James conceded that Traill was "(comparatively)" an "experience" of Perrin's. (Quoted in Hart-Davis, pp. 82–83.)

17. Robert Rogers, *The Double in Literature* (Detroit, 1970). Also helpful are Carl F. Keppler, *The Literature of the Second Self* (Tucson, Arizona, 1972), particularly, and Masao Miyoshi, *The Divided Self* (New York, 1969).

18. Robert Rogers, *ibid.,* pp. 62, 180.

Chapter Three

1. Journal, Sept. 11, 1939. Diary, Jan. 29 and Feb. 4, 1913. Darrell Figgis, "Some Recent Notable Novels," *Nineteenth Century,* LXXIV (Oct., 1913), 792–802. Asa Don Dickinson, *The Best Books of Our Time, 1902–1925* (New York, 1931), pp. 306, 8.

2. Preface, *Fortitude,* Modern Library ed. (New York, 1930), p. vii.

3. Letter to Walpole from London (correspondent's name withheld), Oct. 23, 1929; on file at UTex.

4. Virginia Woolf to Walpole, n.d.; quoted in Hart-Davis, p. 309.

5. For facts about Andersen, Walpole relied on Signe Toksvig, *The Life of Hans Christian Andersen* (New York, 1934), which he identified (Diary, 1934–35, *passim*) as "Tostig."

6. Walpole to Dorothea Walpole, Sept. 4, 1937; on file at UTex.

7. Anon, "New Fiction," *Church Times,* CXVIII (Sept. 3, 1937), 245.

8. "Green Courts," unpublished MS on file at UTex., p. 10.

9. Anon., "New Fiction," *Oxford Chronicle,* June 4, 1909, n.p.

10. Joseph Warren Beach, "The English Sentimentalists," *North American Review,* CCXVI (July, 1922), 95.

11. Anon, "Hugh Walpole," *Times Literary Supplement,* March 7, 1952, p. 172.

12. Besides their setting, *The Inquisitor* and Eliot's *Murder in the Cathedral* are similar structurally, in that the first part is divided from the last by an interlude: by the Archbishop's sermon in the play, and by a letter from the Bishop of Polchester in the novel.

13. "My Most Successful Book," *John O'London's Weekly,* XXXVIII (Oct. 8, 1937), 38.

14. T. S. Eliot, "Tradition and the Individual Talent," *The Sacred Wood* (London, 1920); rptd. in Gerald J. and Nancy M. Goldberg,

eds., *The Modern Critical Spectrum* (Englewood Cliffs, N.J., 1962), pp. 163–64 espec.

Chapter Four

1. "A Prefatory 'Tale,'" *Famous Stories of Five Centuries,* eds. Walpole and Wilfred Partington (New York, [1934]), p. 10; hereafter cited as "Prefatory Tale." "Green Courts," pp. 26–27.

2. Walpole to Henry James, March 15, 1915. On Nov. 12, 1914, he wrote James, "I've given up absolutely any idea of journalism for the present. It's all far too new, too deep, too interesting for me to splash my ignorance upon." (Both letters are quoted in Hart-Davis, pp. 134, 126.)

3. William Gerhardi, whose *Futility* (London, 1922) is a comic novel about the Revolution, was in Russia at the same time as Walpole. Three of the characters in *Futility* are Nina and Vera (sisters) and Vasilievich.

4. Walpole to Henry James, Nov. 12, 1914; quoted in Hart-Davis, p. 125.

5. "A Debt to Dostoevski," London *Times,* July 24, 1925, p. 10; rptd. in *London Mercury,* XII (Oct., 1925), 563. Walpole to Ralph B. Pinker (en re "The German"), Oct. 25, 1939, on file in the Berg Collection, New York Public Library.

6. Walpole to A. S. Frere, Oct. 3, 1934 (excerpt copied into Rupert Hart-Davis' copy of *Captain Nicholas*). Anon., "Richmond Theatre. 'Captain Nicholas' by Leslie Burgess," London *Times,* July 12, 1939, p. 12.

7. Anon., "Escape from Ogre's Castle," *Times Literary Supplement,* Aug. 29, 1936, p. 695.

8. Graham Greene, "Fiction," *Spectator,* CLXIII (Sept. 22, 1939), 420.

9. Anon., *Times Literary Supplement,* Sept. 5, 1942, p. 37. Harold Hobson, "Alas, Sir Hugh!" *Sunday Times* [Aug., 1953], undated clipping in Rupert Hart-Davis' files. Leon Edel, "The Fantasy of *The Killer and the Slain,*" *American Imago,* VIII (Dec., 1951), 351–69, draws some provocative but questionable conclusions about the novel.

10. J. I. M. Stewart, *Eight Modern Writers* (Oxford, 1963), p. 216, puts the date of Conrad's first "wide notice" as 1913. The second and third editions of Walpole's study (1924, 1929) give unfortunately short shrift to the later Conrad novels.

Chapter Five

1. Edward J. Bidwell, "A Twentieth Century Trollope?" *Queen's Quarterly,* XXX (Apr., 1923), 364. Bidwell's thesis is that *The Cathedral* is Greek tragedy.

2. Douglas Newton, "The Book of an Impatient Job," *Bookman* (London), LXIII (Nov., 1922), 102.

3. Steen, pp. 177–78. Clemence Dane, *Tradition and Hugh Walpole* (New York, 1929), p. 188; hereafter cited in the text as "Dane."

4. C. G. Jung to Walpole, Aug. 15, 1930; on file at UTex.

5. A. C. Wilson, "Hugh Walpole's Novels," *Papers of the Manchester Literary Club,* LIII (1927), 178.

6. A short story called "Harmer John: A Portrait" (42 pp.) was written earlier, in June 1919; unpublished MS on file at UTex.

7. Anon., "New Novels," *Times Literary Supplement,* Oct. 21, 1926, p. 718.

8. *Murder in the Cathedral* was presented first in June, 1935; *The Inquisitor* was published in August. See note 12, Chapter 3.

9. "*The Crystal Box,* Glebeshire," *Bookman* (New York), LVII (March, 1923), 41.

10. Walpole to his mother, Aug. (?), 1916; quoted in Hart-Davis, p. 155.

11. Enid Starkie, *From Gautier to Eliot,* 2nd ed. (London, 1962), p. 199. The other English authors she lists are Compton Mackenzie and John Galsworthy.

12. Benn Levy's *Man with Red Hair* (London, 1928) provided starring roles for Charles Laughton and Edward G. Robinson. The Sayler Collection, Lincoln Center Library of the Performing Arts, New York, contains an exhaustive pressbook of the play. *The Old Ladies* (*Night in the House* in America) by Rodney Ackland was produced by John Gielgud with Dame Edith Evans as Agatha Payne. It was published by Victor Gollancz (London, 1935) and Samuel French (New York, 1950).

13. William Lyon Phelps, *As I Like It: Third Series* (New York, 1926), p. 43. L. P. Hartley, "Fiction. The Two Magics," *Spectator,* CXXXIII (Oct. 25, 1924), 612.

14. Anon., *Times Literary Supplement,* May 31, 1928, p. 409.

Chapter Six

1. Henry James, "The Younger Generation," *Times Literary Supplement,* Apr. 2, 1914, p. 157.

2. Anon., "New Novels," London *Times,* July 22, 1938, p. 9.

3. Walpole to Sir Frederick Macmillan, Apr. 18, 1928; the Walpole-Macmillan files are in the British Museum.

4. Anon., "Mr. Walpole's New Novel," *Spectator*, CLX (March 7, 1928), 478. Anon., "Books of the Week. A Minor Vanity Fair," unidentified clipping in Walpole scrapbook, on file at UTex.

5. Anon., "Sir Hugh Walpole," *Manchester Guardian*, June 3, 1941. Walpole wrote reviews and conducted book columns for the following periodicals: London *Evening Standard* (1909–13); *Blue Review* (1913), eds. John Middleton Murry and Katherine Mansfield; New York *Sun* (1919–20); *Vanity Fair* (New York, 1920–23, *passim*); *John O'London's Weekly* (1924–40, *passim*); *New York Herald-Tribune* (1927–34); *Book Society News* (1929–34, rptd. in *Graphic*); and London *Daily Sketch* (1938–41).

6. L. A. G. Strong, "Hugh Walpole: The Making of a Novelist," *John O'London's Weekly*, XLIV (Dec. 20, 1940), 305.

7. "Preface," Sir Walter Scott, *The Waverley Pageant*, eds. Walpole and Wilfred Partington (New York, 1932), pp. xxix, lx.

8. "Prefatory 'Tale,'" p. 20.

9. T. S. Eliot, "Sir Hugh Walpole," London *Times*, June 6, 1941, p. 7. Eliot published the first two chapters of *The Old Ladies* in his magazine *Criterion*, II (Apr., July, 1924), 258–71, 448–59.

10. David Blackwood Paul, "Some Thoughts on Hugh Walpole and the Popular Novel," *Turnbull Library Record*, No. 12 (Sept., 1954), pp. 13, 12, 10.

11. "Jeremy: A Retrospect," unpublished MS on file at UTex., p. 5. The description refers to Roger Kenrick in the unpublished fragment "The Crabtree," also at UTex.

12. "City Under Fire," unpublished MS fragment on file at UTex., pp. 10, 36.

13. Lady Dorothy Nevill, *Leaves from the Note-Books* . . . , ed. Ralph Nevill (London, 1907), pp. 315–16.

Chapter Seven

1. "Foreword," [Thomas Gray,] *Gray's Elegy Written in a Country Churchyard* (London, 1938), pp. xiii–xiv.

2. Author and play appear spurious. Walpole himself wrote at least half the epigraphs for his own books and attributed them to nonexistent sources.

3. Doubleday, Doran advertisement, *Publishers' Weekly*, CXV (Feb. 16, 1929), 714. The deadline was March 3; happy the contestant with access to the *Times Literary Supplement* for Feb. 28, giving the answer!

4. Walpole to Sir Frederick Macmillan, Apr. 1, 1929.

5. Christie, Manson and Woods, Ltd., *Catalogue of the Final Portion of the Famous Library of the Late Sir Hugh Walpole, C. B. E.* (London, 1946), p. 18, item 176.

6. L. C. Hartley, "We Call Upon Hugh Walpole," *Sewanee Review,* XL (July, 1932), 338.

7. "Living in the Lakes has unquestionably changed my feeling about the South. I find it too tame" (Diary, Sept. 7, 1924).

8. Gerald Gould, "Mr. Walpole and Others," *Observer,* March 23, 1930, p. 8. L. A. G. Strong, "A Glorious Saga of the Lakes," Reprint Society (London) *Broadsheet,* Feb., 1955, p. 1.

9. Marjorie Bowen, "Mr. Walpole's Latest," London *Morning Post,* March 18, 1930, p. 15. Gerald Gould, *ibid.*

10. Anon., "Book Page," Sioux City *Journal,* Apr. 3, 1932, p. 8.

11. Anon., "Mr. Hugh Walpole's New Romance," London *Times,* March 18, 1930, p. 10.

12. Hubert H. Dumville, "The Herries Saga: An Introduction," unpublished MS in Mr. Dumville's possession, p. 19.

13. Walpole to Sir Frederick Macmillan, Oct. 24, 1929.

14. Roger Pippett, "Our Champion Word-Spinster," London *Daily Herald,* Aug. 28, 1932.

15. When MGM filmed *Vanessa,* the censor deleted the extramarital idyll, to Walpole's disgust (Diary, Sept. 20, 1934). Despite a notable cast (Helen Hayes played Vanessa), a talented director (David Selznick), and high production costs, the film did poorly, as Walpole had foreseen.

16. Hart-Davis, *passim;* also Robin Maugham, *Somerset and All the Maughams* (New York, 1966); Beverley Nichols, *A Case of Human Bondage* (London, 1966); and Alec Waugh, "The Nail in the Coffin," *Harper's Magazine,* CCVII (July, 1953), 32–37 (rptd. in *My Brother Evelyn and Other Profiles* [London, 1968], pp. 128–40).

17. "Willie at his nicest as he always is with me" (Diary, June 16, 1918). See also Walpole, "William Somerset Maugham," *Vanity Fair,* Jan., 1920, p. 47; rptd. in *Cavalcade of the 1920's and 1930's,* eds. Cleveland Amory and Frederick Bradlee (London, 1961), pp. 40–41. Concerning the first night of Maugham's play *Love in a Cottage* Walpole once assured Arnold Bennett, "Maugham will be hurt for ever if I don't go" (Jan. 21, 1918; on file at Bennett Museum, Burslem, Stoke-on-Trent).

18. P. G. Wodehouse, *Author! Author!* (New York, 1962), p. 79.

19. Richard Cordell, *W. Somerset Maugham* (London, 1937), p. 127, paraphrasing *Romeo and Juliet.*

20. James Agate, *Ego 5* (London, 1942), p. 98. "Notes from a Northern Cottage," *Golden Book,* XII (Dec., 1930), 41.

21. Somerset Maugham, Introduction, *Cakes and Ale,* Modern Library ed. (New York, 1950); rptd. as "For Maugham It's 'Cakes and Ale,'" *New York Times Book Review,* March 19, 1950, pp. 1, 38.

22. Walpole to Francis Brett Young, Oct. 23, 1931; on file at the University of Birmingham, England.

23. Elinor Mordaunt, *Gin and Bitters* (New York, 1931); rptd. as *The Full Circle* (London, 1931).

24. C. H., "'Gin and Bitters,'" London *Daily Mail,* n.d. [1931], clipping in Walpole scrapbook, on file at UTex.

25. Preface, *Mr. Perrin and Mr. Traill,* Everyman ed. (London, 1935), p. x.

26. V. S. Pritchett, "New Novels," *New Statesman and Nation,* XIV (Sept. 11, 1937), 378.

27. The Dedicatory Letter concludes with an acknowledgment to "*The Tragedy of Fotheringhay,* by the Hon. Mrs. Maxwell-Scott—a delightful and thrilling work."

28. Anon., "The Ancestors of Sir Hugh Walpole," *The Cantuarian,* XXIV (July, 1952). Though accused of heresy, Robin Herries is not a Jesuit.

29. J. E. Cirlot, *A Dictionary of Symbols,* trans. Jack Sage (New York, 1962), *passim.*

30. Richard G. Burnett, "The Courage of Hugh Walpole," *London Quarterly Review,* CLXVI (Oct., 1941), 463.

Chapter Eight

1. *Golden Scarecrow* and *Thirteen Travellers,* collections of short stories with a common theme and setting, are discussed in Chapters 5 and 6, respectively.

2. "The Monkaster Feast" is in the "Social Monthly," I (1901), juvenilia on file at UTex. For details on the other stories see Bibliography.

3. "The Silver Mask" attained renown as the basis of an excellent play, *Kind Lady* by Edward Chodorov and George Haight. It opened in New York, April, 1935, with Grace George; in London, June, 1936, with Sybil Thorndike. A 1951 film version, with Ethel Barrymore, Maurice Evans, Angela Lansbury, and Keenan Wynn, was also well received.

4. ". . . Mr. Montmorency whom [the critics] are all praising is entirely imagined. There was never any Mr. Montmorency!" (Journal, March 17, 1940). Hart-Davis, pp. 76, 401, points out that both the lost fountain and the earlier trip to Rome are also fictitious.

5. For minor autobiographical pieces, see Bibliography.

6. *Open Letter of an Optimist* (1941) contains Walpole's strongest condemnation of the English public schools.

7. *My Religious Experience* (1928) puts Walpole's missionary year in proper context.

8. James Agate, "Some New Books. Lovely," London *Daily Express,* Dec. 29, 1932, p. 4.

9. Dane, pp. 197–98, 205–6.

10. "Billy's Christmas Eve" (see Bibliography).

11. Anon., "Other-Worldly Tales" (review of *Head in Green Bronze*), London *Times,* Feb. 25, 1938, p. 10.

12. "Thirty Years a Novelist," *Listener,* XVIII (Nov. 24, 1937), 1121.

Chapter Nine

1. Letters from Conrad to Walpole, reprinted in Hart-Davis; in Walpole's diary, *passim,* he records warm comments from Conrad on all of Walpole's novels from *The Dark Forest* to the time of Conrad's death. Conrad's greatest enthusiasm was for *The Secret City.*

2. For the contents, chosen by Walpole, see Bibliography. J. M. Dent, *Memoirs . . . 1849–1926* (London, 1928), p. 236, discusses the King's Treasuries of Literature series, to which the anthology belongs.

3. W. L. George, "Who Is the Man?," *Bookman* (New York), XXXVIII (Feb., 1914), 655–62; rptd. in *Literary Chapters* (Boston, 1918), pp. 44–73.

4. In Edward J. O'Brien, ed., *Best British Short Stories of 1926* (New York, 1926), pp. 424–25.

5. Susan Sontag, "Literature," *The Great Ideas Today: 1966,* eds. Robert M. Hutchins and Mortimer J. Adler (Chicago, 1966), pp. 154–55.

6. Walpole to Edward Marsh, Apr. 14, 1911, [Feb., 1914], Oct. 9, 1920, July 25, 1921, Sept. 3, 1921, in the Berg Collection, New York Public Library. J. B. Pinker to Sir Frederick Macmillan, Aug. 14, 1917. Lovat Dickson, *The House of Words* (New York, 1963), pp. 271–73. Walpole to Thomas Mark, Jan. 19, 1941. Walpole to Harold Macmillan, Nov. 23, 1937; rptd. in Simon Nowell-Smith, ed., *Letters to Macmillan* (London, 1967), pp. 324–25.

7. J. B. Priestley, *Margin Released* (New York, 1963), p. 175.

Selected Bibliograpy

PRIMARY SOURCES

1. Novels. The Cumberland Edition. Special Prefaces by the author. London: Macmillan, 1934. All novels and short-story collections through *Above the Dark Circus* (1931), except *Rogue Herries*. Added to the Cumberland Edition later were: in 1937, *All Souls' Night, Captain Nicholas;* 1938, *The Inquisitor;* 1940, *A Prayer for My Son, John Cornelius.*
2. Collections. All novels, with their original dates, are listed in the Chronology.

All Souls' Night. London: Macmillan, 1933. ("The Whistle," "The Silver Mask," "The Staircase," "A Carnation for an Old Man," "Tarnhelm," "Mr. Oddy," "Seashore Macabre," "Lilac," "The Oldest Talland," "The Little Ghost," "Mrs. Lunt," "Sentimental but True," "Portrait in Shadow," "The Snow," "The Ruby Glass," "Spanish Dusk").

"The City Under Fire." (On file at UTex.) Unpublished fragment, 1941. ("Proem," "Miss Rendal").

Four Fantastic Tales. Special Preface by the author. London: Macmillan, 1932. (*Maradick at Forty, The Prelude to Adventure, Portrait of a Man with Red Hair, Above the Dark Circus*).

Head in Green Bronze. London: Macmillan, 1938. ("Head in Green Bronze," "The German," "The Exile," "The Train," "The Haircut," "Let the Bores Tremble," "The Honey-Box," "The Fear of Death," "Field with Five Trees," "Having No Hearts," "The Conjurer").

The Herries Chronicle. Special Preface by the author. London: Macmillan, 1939. (*Rogue Herries, Judith Paris, The Fortress, Vanessa*).

A Hugh Walpole Anthology. Preface by Joseph Conrad. London: Dent, 1921. King's Treasuries of Literature Series. ("Some Children" [from *Jeremy, The Golden Scarecrow*], "Men and Women" [from *Mr. Perrin and Mr. Traill, Fortitude, The Green Mirror, The Captives*], "London" [from *Fortitude, The Duchess of Wrexe, The Green Mirror, The Captives*], "Country Places" [from *The Wooden Horse, Maradick at Forty, The Green Mirror*], "Russia" [from *The Dark Forest, The Secret City*].

The Jeremy Stories. London: Macmillan, 1941. (*Jeremy, Jeremy and Hamlet, Jeremy at Crale*).

Selected Bibliography

Mr. Huffam. London: Macmillan, 1948. ("The White Cat," "The Train to the Sea," "The Perfect Close," "Service for the Blind," "The Faithful Servant," "Miss Thom," "Women Are Motherly," "The Beard," "The Last Trump," "Green Tie," "The Church in the Snow," "Mr. Huffam").

"Mrs. Comber at Rafiel." (On file at UTex.) Unpublished MS, 1912; stories published separately. ("Rain," "Sentimental but True," "The Oldest Talland").

New Story Reader 13, 14, 15. London: Macmillan, [1940]. (*Jeremy,* Chaps. I, II; VIII, X; III, V).

The Silver Thorn. London: Macmillan, 1928. ("The Little Donkeys with the Crimson Saddles," "The Enemy in Ambush," "Chinese Horses," "A Silly Old Fool," "Ecstasy," "The Tarn," "No Unkindness Intended," "The Etching," "Major Wilbraham," "The Enemy," "Old Elizabeth," "A Picture," "The Dove," "The Tiger," "Bachelors"). The stories in the American edition (New York: Doubleday, Doran, 1928) have a different order.

"Waring." (On file at UTex.) Unpublished MS, 1914. ("The Adventure of Mrs. Comber's Birthday" [published], "Elsie March," "Mrs. Comber," "Maradick").

3. Uncollected Short Stories, Published and Unpublished.

"The Adventure of Mrs. Comber's Birthday," *Argosy Magazine,* Jan., 1933, pp. 47–54.

"The Adventure of the Riotous Children," *Book News Monthly,* XXXII (Apr., 1914), [374–79]. [Originally in "Waring," *q.v. supra;* missing from MS.]

"Billy's Christmas Eve." ("Adapted from Hugh Walpole.") London: Blackie, 1934. Blackie's Graded Story Readers Series.

"The Brother," *Yale Review,* XXIII (Sept., 1933), 139–59; *Storyteller* (London), March, 1934.

"The Clocks," *Fortnightly Review,* C (Oct., 1913), 778–87.

"The Critic," *Saturday Review* (England), CXVIII (July 11, 1914), 42–43; *Smart Set* (America), LXIII (Dec., 1920), 23–25.

"The Dog and the Dragon," *Windsor Magazine,* LVIII (Oct., 1923), 475–83.

"The Girl Who Was Herself," *Hearst's International,* XLVII (Jan., 1925), 76–79, 127–28.

"Giving Up," *Smart Set,* (July, 1910), 55–63.

"The Green Shining Tree," *Harper's Bazaar* (New York), LXIV (Aug., 1930), 87, 92, 94.

"Half Way Upstairs," *Strand Magazine,* June, 1940, pp. 107–13.

"Harmer John. A Portrait." Unpublished MS, 1919. (On file UTex.)

"A Harmless Flirt," *Cosmopolitan*, LXXXI (July, 1926), 100–103, 118, 120, 122, 124; as "Golden Dust," *Nash's–Pall Mall Magazine*, LXXVIII (Dec., 1926), 22–25, 123–24, 126, 128.

"Jimmy in Search of a Hero." Unpublished MS, 1906. (On file UTex.)

"A Little Cure for Bachelors," *London Magazine*, XLVIII (March, 1922), 24–33; *Chicago Tribune*, Oct. 1, 1922.

"Miss Finchley's Hour," *Good Housekeeping* (New York), LXXIX (Dec., 1924), 14–19.

"Monsieur Felicité," *English Review*, VI (Sept., 1910), 256–69; *Living Age* (New York), CCLXVII (Oct. 8, 1910), 100–108.

"Mother's a Pity," *Collier's*, CI (Jan. 8, 1938), 9–11, 32–34.

"Mrs. Comber at Rafiel," *Storyteller* (London), Aug., 1921, pp. 453–59. (On file UTex. under title "Rain" in collection "Mrs. Comber at Rafiel," *q.v. supra*).

"Portrait of Menzies," *Strand Magazine*, XC (Feb., 1936), 418–27.

"Red Amber," *Windsor Magazine*, LIX (Dec., 1923), 21–27.

"Single Women," *T. P.'s Christmas Issue*, 1913.

"Slippers," *Liberty Magazine*, XIX (July 19, 1924), 32–37.

"Snow on the Hills," *American Magazine*, CXXV (Feb., 1938), 28–30, 156–58.

"A Stranger." Oxford: Blackwell, [1926]. "Jolly Books" ser.

"Turnip-Lanterns." Unpublished MS, [1913?]. (On file UTex.)

"The Twisted Inn," *Smart Set*, XLVI (June, 1915), 245–51.

"Under the Colossi," *Nash's–Pall Mall Magazine*, LXXVI (Dec., 1925), 26–29, 108, 110, 113.

"Young Jacob," *London Magazine*, June, 1913. (I haven't seen this item.)

4. Juvenilia. (Unpublished MSS, on file UTex.)

a. Novels:

"Arnado the Fearless," ("By W. LeQuensc"), March, 1899; "At the Sound of the Trump," May, 1899; "A Baron's Daughter," 1899; "Chronicles of a Lady of Charles I," n.d.: "Chronicles of Shipington," 1899; "Colchester Manor," 1897; "For the Sake of the King," unfinished, 1899; "A Golden Ladder," n.d.; "In the Days of Queen Mary," n.d.; "Ornod, the Viking or Pabo, the Monk," [1901–02]; "Strafford," unfinished, 1900, cont. in "Social Monthly," Vol. II; "Sword of Damocles," n.d.; "True and Brave," 1898.

b. Play:

"Zinthe and Agonistas," n.d.

c. Collections:

[Bede College Notebooks.] 4 vols., illus.: I, "Serials," Aug., 1901–Feb., 1902; II, III, IV, "The Book," Aug.–Dec., 1901, Jan.–

March, 1902, Apr.–May, 1902. Also unnumbered, untitled note-book, 1898.

"Christmas Miscellany." 2 vols., illus. [by Hugh and Dorothea Walpole]. 1901, 1902.

"Social Monthly" ("The Social Miscellany," "Social Fortnightly"). 2 vols., illus. 1898–1900.

d. Special diary:

"The Spanish-American War." Unfinished, illus. [1898?].

5. Selected Nonfiction.

a. Cited in text.

Anthony Trollope. London: Macmillan, 1928. "English Men of Letters" ser.

The Apple Trees. Waltham, St. Lawrence, Berks.: Golden Cockerel, 1932.

The Cathedral (play). London: Macmillan, 1937.

The Crystal Box. Glasgow: Robert MacLehose, 1924. In *Bookman* (New York), LVI–LVII (Oct., 1922–May, 1923), *passim;* rptd. in *T. P.'s and Cassell's Weekly,* n.s. III (Dec. 6, 1924–March 28, 1925), *passim.*

The English Novel. Cambridge: University Press, 1925. The 1925 Rede Lecture.

"Foreword." [Thomas Gray], *Gray's Elegy Written in a Country Churchyard.* London: Limited Editions Club, 1938, pp. v–xv.

Joseph Conrad. London: Nisbet, [1916]; 2nd ed., 1924; 3rd ed., 1929. "Writers of the Day" ser.

A Letter to a Modern Novelist. London: Hogarth, 1932.

"My Most Successful Book," *John O'London's Weekly,* XXXVIII (Oct. 8, 1937), 37–40.

My Religious Experience. London: Ernest Benn, 1928. "Affirmations" ser. In *Delineator,* CXII (May, 1928), 19, 62, as "My Religious Life."

Open Letter of an Optimist. London: Macmillan, 1941.

"Preface." Anon., *Out of the Deep: Letters from Soviet Timber Camps* (London: Geoffrey Bles, 1933).

"A Prefatory 'Tale,' " in Walpole and Wilfred Partington, eds., *Famous Stories of Five Centuries.* New York: Farrar and Rinehart, [1934], pp. 5–21.

Reading: An Essay. New York and London: Harper, 1926. "These Diversions" ser.

Roman Fountain. London: Macmillan, 1940.

"Sir Walter Scott." Walter Scott, *The Waverley Pageant,* eds. Walpole and Wilfred Partington. New York and London: Harper, 1932, pp. ix–xl; and section prefaces, *passim.*

b. Recommended, but not cited in text.

"A Creator" (Charles Laughton), *Week-End Review,* I (May 10, 1930), 302.
"Critic and Novelist," *Bookman* (New York), LXIII (Apr., 1926), 140–45.
"An English Lady" (Mrs. Walpole), *Fortnightly Review,* CXXVIII (Sept., 1927), 289–97; rptd. in W. J. Margetson, ed., *G. H. S. Walpole: Bishop of Edinburgh* (Paisley, Renfrewshire, Scotland: Alexander Gardner, 1930), pp. 46ff.
"Grock," *New Statesman,* XII (Nov. 2, 1918), 91–92.
"The Historical Novel in England Since Sir Walter Scott," in H. J. C. Grierson, ed., *Sir Walter Scott To-Day* (London: Constable, 1932), pp. 161–88.
"Introduction." Hubert Henry Davies, *The Plays* . . . (London: Chatto and Windus, 1921), Vol. I, pp. v–xx.
"John Galsworthy," in W. R. Inge, ed., *The Post Victorians* (London: Ivor Nicholson and Watson, 1933), pp. 173–85.
"Living with Beautiful Things," *Delineator,* CXIV (Feb., 1929), 7, 76, 78.
"My Father," in W. J. Margetson, ed., *G. H. S. Walpole* (see "An English Lady," *supra*), pp. 37–45.
"Novels Thick and Thin," *Listener,* XXI (Feb. 2, 1939), 272.
"Why Didn't I Put Poison in His Coffee?" (Hitler), *John O'London's Weekly,* XLIV (Oct. 11, 1940), [25]–26.

SECONDARY SOURCES

Anon. "Obituary, Sir Hugh Walpole," *Times Literary Supplement,* June 7, 1941, p. 277. Not the misleading *Times* obituary of June 2. Good tracing of Walpole's literary forbears. Shaky psychoanalysis.
BEACH, JOSEPH WARREN. "The English Sentimentalists," *North American Review,* CCXVI (July, 1922), [89]–101. Walpole as the "first great triumph, the imaginative genius" of the new English sentimental school.
———. "Proud Words" and "Sawing the Air," *Atlantic Monthly,* CXXXII (Oct., Nov., 1923), 511–15, 629–33. Rptd. in *The Outlook for American Prose.* Chicago: Univ. of Chicago Press, [1926] pp. 109–21, 125–36. Attacks Walpole *et al.* for "precious" diction, careless imagery, overemphatic love scenes.
———. *The Twentieth Century Novel: Studies in Technique.* New York: D. Appleton-Century, 1932. Walpole, as "sentimental subjectivist," compared and contrasted with Edith Wharton, another Henry James protégé.

Selected Bibliography

BENNETT, ARNOLD. "Hugh Walpole, A Familiar Sketch," *Book News Monthly*, XXXII (Apr., 1914), [371]–72. Abridged as "A Familiar Sketch of Walpole." *Hugh Walpole, Master Novelist*. New York: George H. Doran, [1914], pp. 16–22. Further abridged as "Hugh Walpole, the Person," [Grant Overton, ed.], *Hugh Walpole, Appreciation*. New York: George H. Doran, [1923?], pp. 2–4. Lively appraisal of Walpole to 1914, particularly *Perrin* and *Fortitude*. Some factual errors.

BESCOU, YVES. "Une Famille anglaise de 1720 à 1920," *Revue de l'Enseignement des Langues Vivantes*, LV (Nov., 1938), 385–93. Leisurely but thorough analysis of pace and character in main Herries tetralogy.

BIDWELL, EDWARD J. "A Twentieth Century Trollope?" *Queen's Quarterly*, XXX (Apr., 1923), 363–71. Refutes a common epithet by analyzing *Cathedral* as Greek tragedy.

COLLIER, JOHN. "The Late Hugh Walpole, Esquire," *Time and Tide* (London), XIV (Oct. 14, 1933), 231–32. Title ironic, referring to Steen biography. Excellent analysis of its weaknesses, and of Walpole's strengths, newfound in Herries books.

COVENEY, PETER. *Poor Monkey: The Child in Literature*. London: Rockliff, 1957. Psychoanalyzes Jeremy books and *Golden Scarecrow*. Presumptive.

DANE, CLEMENCE. *Tradition and Hugh Walpole*. New York: Doubleday, Doran, 1929. Walpole as a "traditive." Miss Dane unconvincingly uses "allegory," "symbolism" and "underplot" as synonyms for Walpole's "innovation in idea which modernized [the] old-fashioned tale." Last half gives plots of Walpole novels (minus the Russian ones) through 1928. Diffuse.

DOTTIN, PAUL. "L'oeuvre de Hugh Walpole," *Revue de France*, Douzième Année, I (1 Feb., 1932), 560–67. Favorable survey with reservations. Notes paucity of French editions.

DUMVILLE, HUBERT H. "The Herries Saga: An Introduction." Unpublished MS, July, 1937. On file with Mr. Dumville, whose stated aim was "to stimulate an appetite among the public to read the four volumes." The Herries books as fitted to a moral and religious framework. Gives plot highlights, useful details of Cumberland area.

DUTTON, GEORGE B. "Romance and Mr. Walpole," *Sewanee Review*, XXXI (Apr., 1923), 178–86. On Walpole's "different" books— *Captives* and *Cathedral*. Contrasts his Realism with others' Naturalism. Helpful.

EDEL, LEON. "Hugh Walpole and Henry James: The Fantasy of *The Killer and the Slain*," *American Imago*, VIII (Dec., 1951), 351–

69. Important as the only full-fledged psychoanalysis of a Walpole work, but conclusions open to question.

GILLETT, ERIC. "Peter Pan, Novelist," *National and English Review,* CXXXVIII (Apr., 1951), 233–36. Favorable review-article of Hart-Davis biography. Competent on Walpole.

HART-DAVIS, RUPERT. *Hugh Walpole, A Biography.* London and New York: Macmillan, 1952. The official "Life" deputed by Walpole. Not literary criticism but a monument of organization carved with patience, tact, humor and sensibility from the mountain of material extant on one of the busiest authors in our century. Invaluable.

HERGESHEIMER, JOSEPH. *Hugh Walpole, An Appreciation.* New York: George H. Doran, 1919. Abridged in [Grant Overton, ed.], *Hugh Walpole, Appreciations* (see Bennett, *supra*), pp. 5–18. Commissioned as a souvenir booklet, thus necessarily a whitewash. Discussion limited to *Secret City, Golden Scarecrow, Green Mirror.* Some good insights.

JAMES, HENRY. "The Younger Generation," *Times Literary Supplement,* March 19, Apr. 2, 1914, pp. 133–34, 157–58; rptd., revised, as "The New Novel," *Notes on Novelists.* New York: Scribner's, 1914, pp. 314–61. Exalted because of its author. Walpole's "freshness" a curse and a blessing, but Walpole better than E. M. Forster and D. H. Lawrence. Emphasizes *Duchess of Wrexe.*

JOHNSON, PAMELA HANSFORD. "Literature." *The Baldwin Age,* John Raymond, ed. Chester Springs, Pa.: Dufour, 1961, pp. 179–88. Scattered, pungent comments on Walpole as important to and typical of literary conventionalism, 1923–37.

JOHNSON, R. BRIMLEY. "Hugh Walpole." *Some Contemporary Novelists (Men).* London: Leonard Parsons, 1922, pp. 53–78. Walpole "born mature" as novelist. Plot of all the novels to 1922.

KNICKERBOCKER, WILLIAM S. "Analysis of Hugh Walpole's *Rogue Herries," Creative Reading,* IV (June, 1930), 366–80. Thorough dissection. Fault-finding, but several worthwhile points.

LOWNDES, MARIE [ADELAIDE] BELLOC. "Hugh Walpole," *Book News Monthly,* XXXII (Apr., 1914), 372–73. Abridged as "Walpole the Man," *Hugh Walpole, Master Novelist* (see Bennett, *supra*), pp. 23–26. Gentler, more laudatory companion to Bennett essay.

MANN, DOROTHEA LAWRENCE. "Hugh Walpole Comes Again to America," *Boston Evening Transcript,* Dec. 18, 1926, Book Section, p. 1. Combines interview, personality analysis, summary of books to date.

MANNING, ETHEL. "Characterizations in Ten of Hugh Walpole's Novels." Unpublished MA Thesis, Univ. of Texas, 1938. Thumbnail sketches, from sociological angle, of *Maradick, Fortitude,*

Young Enchanted, Green Mirror, Captives, Gods and Mr. Perrin, Wooden Horse, Duchess of Wrexe, Dark Forest, Cathedral. Useful statistics.

MORGAN, LOUISE. "Hugh Walpole Finds Himself," *Everyman,* n.s. V (June 4, 1931), 587–89. Unusually good interview concerning work habits and views on the novel in general.

MURRY, JOHN MIDDLETON. "The Case of Mr. Hugh Walpole," *Nation and Athenaeum,* XXIX (July 16, 1921), 584–85. Perceptive analysis of Walpole's early reading public.

PAUL, DAVID BLACKWOOD. "Some Thoughts on Hugh Walpole and the Popular Novel," *Turnbull Library Record,* No. 12 (Sept., 1954), pp. 3–20. Second Memorial Lecture under Hugh Walpole Memorial Fund established by Miss Julie Tomlinson. Walpole's anti-intellectual "treatment of authors and literature generally as shown in his novels, and the influence that treatment had on popular thought." Stern but just.

PRIESTLEY, J[OHN] B[OYNTON]. "Hugh Walpole," *English Journal,* XVII (Sept., 1928), 529–36. Walpole as mixture of Trollope and Dostoevski.

———. "Hugh Walpole, Novelist," *Bookman* (New York), LXIV (Feb., 1927), 684–92; rptd., revised, in *Fortnightly Review,* CXXVIII (Dec., 1927), 753–63. Able survey emphasizing variety and Russian influences.

[SADLEIR, MICHAEL.] "Walpole, Sir Hugh Seymour," *Dictionary of National Biography. 1941–1950.* Eds. L. G. Wickham Legg and E. T. Williams. London: Oxford Univ. Press, 1959, pp. 920–23. Solid review of literary and personal qualities.

STEELE, ELIZABETH. *Hugh Walpole: His World of Fiction.* Ann Arbor, Mich.: University Microfilms, 1967. Thorough examination of novels and short stories, published and still in manuscript, including juvenilia. Documentary sidelights.

STEEN, MARGUERITE. *Hugh Walpole: A Study.* London: Ivor Nicholson and Watson, 1933. Less a scholarly work than a rhapsodic fantasy portraying Walpole as a religious Romantic. Laudable chapter on the collected short stories.

STRONG, L[EONARD] A[LFRED] G[EORGE]. "Hugh Walpole," *Time and Tide* (London), XXV (June 17, 1944), 532–33. Partly biographical. Stresses Walpole's belief in Evil.

———. "Hugh Walpole: The Making of a Novelist," *John O'London's Weekly,* XLIV (Dec. 20, 1940), [305]–6. Competent overview of Walpole as critic, lecturer, and mood-driven thinker.

———. *Personal Remarks.* London: Peter Nevill, 1953. Final distillation of Strong's articles on Walpole, *q.v.* Good source.

————. "Two Romantic Novelists" (Walpole and Francis Brett Young), *Teachers' World and Schoolmistress*, Vol. XLV, Sept. 15, 1937. "One of the most understanding [critiques] I've ever had" (Walpole, Journal). Walpole as a "romantic . . . liberating the less conscious levels of the mind," especially fear, through his writings.

SWINNERTON, FRANK. *Figures in the Foreground.* New York: Doubleday, 1964. Valuable description of literary *ambience* against background of Walpole-Swinnerton letters. Little criticism.

WALL, ARNOLD. *Sir Hugh Walpole and His Writings.* Wellington, N. Z.: Turnbull Library, 1947. First Memorial Lecture (see Paul, *supra*). Useful tabulations. Walpole as a Romantic. Laudatory.

WALPOLE, DOROTHEA. "Notes About a Father and a Brother." Unpublished MS on file at UTex, n.d. [post-1940]. Important family source.

WILSON, A. C. "Hugh Walpole's Novels," *Papers of the Manchester Literary Club*, LIII (1927), [171]–88. Layman's overview, alert, naive, informal.

Index

Agate, James, 17, 128, 140
Andersen, Hans Christian, 48, 155
Austen, Jane, 18, 118, 143
Authority figures (motif), 142–44

Balzac, Honoré de, 51, 112
Barham, Richard Harris ("Thomas Ingoldsby"), 18
Barrymore, Ethel, 160
Beach, Joseph Warren, 52–53, 147
Beards (motif), 142
Becket, Thomas à, 74, 85
Bennett, Arnold, 12, 159; as novelist, 18, 21, 151; as friend, 19, 34, 140, 147, 148; as critic, 20, 34, 44, 154
Beowulf, 110
Beresford, J. D., 149, 153
Besier, Rudolf, 154
Bidwell, Edward J., 73
Blake, William, 132
Bloomsbury, 43, 94, 105, 106, 116
Blue Review, The, 158
Boer War, 96, 126
Bowen, Elizabeth, 21, 148
Bowen, Marjorie, 121
Brett Young, Francis, 129, 153
Brontë, Charlotte, 23, 81–82, 110, 147
Brontë, Emily, 23, 51, 147
Browning, Robert, 71, 110
Bulwer-Lytton, Edward, 26
Burgess, Leslie, 66
Burnett, Richard G., 133

Caesar, Julius, 114
Cambridge University, 18, 27, 77–79, 109
Cannan, Gilbert, 153

Carlyle, Thomas, 110
Case of Human Bondage, A, by Beverley Nichols, 159
"Cathédrale Engloutie, La," by Claude Debussy, 74
Cats (motif), 121, 144
Chandos-Poole, Lady Anna, 95, 106
Chaplin, Charlie, 19
Chaucer, Geoffrey, 108, 142
Chekhov, Anton, 136, 137, 138
Chesterton, G. K., 109
Clocks (motif), 143–44
Coleridge, Samuel Taylor, 119
Connolly, Cyril, 38
Conrad, Joseph, as novelist, 17, 71–72, 156; *The Secret Agent* and *Fortitude*, 51; as friend, 71; *Nostromo*, 71; in *Joseph Conrad*, 71–72, 91, 93, 107, 153, 156; Richard Curle on, 72, 93; writes preface to *Hugh Walpole Anthology*, 147, 148; likes *Secret City*, 161
Cordell, Richard, 128
Cornwall, 28–38, 42–44, 46–47, 82–83, 87, 120, 134, 137
Crawford, F. Marion, 26, 110, 116
Cromwell, Oliver, 114, 134
Cumberland, *see* Lake Country
Curle, Richard, 72, 93

Dane, Clemence (Winifred Ashton), 11, 33, 78, 142–43, 147
De la Mare, Walter, 111
De Maupassant, Guy, 136, 137
Dickens, Charles, 22, 23, 147; *David Copperfield*, 17, 51, 153; *Nicholas Nickleby*, 35; as model, 51, 52
Dickson, Lovat, 149

Divided Self, The, by Masao Miyoshi, 155
Dogs (motif), 25, 121, 144
Doppelgänger, *see* "Pursued-Protagonist Pattern"
Doran, George H., 18, 148
Dostoevski, Feodor, 55, 63, 71, 77, 78
Double in Literature, The, by Robert Rogers, 41
Dumville, Hubert H., 12, 159
Durham, England, 19, 73, 87, 139, 140

Eliot, George (Mary Ann Evans), 22, 143, 147
Eliot, T. S., as critic, 20; defends imitation, 53–54; *Murder in the Cathedral,* 53, 85, 155, 157; and *Inquisitor,* 53, 155; *Waste Land,* 107; defends Walpole, 110; publishes some of *Old Ladies,* 158
"Elizabeth" (Gräfin von Arnim), 19, 28
Epsom College, 34
Evans, Dame Edith, 157
Evans, Maurice, 160

Falkner, Meade, 73
"Fantasy of *The Killer and the Slain,* The," by Leon Edel, 156
Faulkner, William, 148
Fielding, Henry, 22, 51, 108, 112, 147
Flaubert, Gustav, 72, 136, 137
Forster, E. M., precedes Walpole as tutor, 19, 28; Henry James on, 20; helps with *Wooden Horse,* 28, 149; *Where Angels Fear to Tread* and *Room with a View,* 51; influence on *Maradick* and *Prelude to Adventure,* 51, 52; *Longest Journey,* 52
Frere, A. S., 65
Frost, Robert, 127

Galsworthy, John, 18, 21, 52, 151, 157
Garnett, Constance, 55

Gaskell, Elizabeth, 26, 27
George, Grace, 160
George, W. L., 147, 153
Germany, 18, 19, 64, 66, 70, 71
Gielgud, John, 157
Gissing, George, 23, 81
Glasgow, Ellen, 109
Glebeshire, 49, 69, 81, 87, 120, 139
Goldsmith, Oliver, 23
Gould, Gerald, 121
Gray, Thomas, 119
Greene, Graham, 21, 69, 151

Hardy, Thomas, 22, 81, 82, 127, 128, 130, 140
Hart-Davis, Sir Rupert, as friend and biographer, 11, 12; Thomas Mark to, 116; Walpole to, 126; *Hugh Walpole, A Biography,* quoted, 21, 42, 44, 58, 126, 128, 135, 138, 146; on Virginia Woolf, 21, 127; on Somerset Maugham, 127, 128; on *Bright Pavilions,* 133
Harte, Bret, 136
Hartley, L. C., 119–20
Hartley, L. P., 91
Hawthorne, Nathaniel, 27, 136, 137
Hayes, Helen, 159
Hazlitt, William, 110
Hemingway, Ernest, 19, 115
Henry, O. (William Sydney Porter), 136, 137
Hergesheimer, Joseph, 147
Hitler, Adolf, 19, 63–64, 70, 144
Hobson, Harold, 69
Hollywood, 17, 48, 50, 65, 67, 87, 137, 149, 153, 159
Horses (motif), 132–33, 141
Huxley, Aldous, 105, 106, 107, 109

Ingoldsby Legends, The, by Richard Harris Barham, 18
Irving, Washington, 17

James, G. P. R., 26, 110
James, Henry, 17, 124; as friend, 19, 20, 139; essay "The Younger Generation," 20, 95, 147–48; *Green Mirror* and *Duchess of Wrexe* as

"Jamesian," 25, 52, 81, 95–96; criticizes *Maradick, Perrin, Fortitude,* 30, 31, 39, 44, 155; as "Henry Galleon," 51; *Golden Bowl,* 52, 96; Walpole writes from Russia, 55–56, 59; likes *Duchess of Wrexe,* 95; *Turn of the Screw,* 98; Walpole writes of, 139, 140; "Henry James's High Hat" (*Apple Trees*), 140; his letters quoted, 30, 39, 155

James Tait Black Memorial Prize, 55
John O'London's Weekly, 158
Johnson, Pamela Hansford, 151
Joyce, James, 17, 18, 21, 105, 106, 107, 109, 136, 147, 148
Jung, Carl, 79, 133

Kaye-Smith, Sheila, 153
Keats, John, 110
King's School, Canterbury, 19, 73, 85, 89, 126, 154
Kipling, Rudyard, 17, 23

Lake Country, 66, 106, 117, 119, 120, 122, 124, 140
Lamb, Charles, 110
Landor, Walter Savage, 110
Lansbury, Angela, 160
Laughton, Charles, 157
Lawrence, D. H., 11, 17, 18, 20, 44, 105, 107, 109, 136
Life of Hans Christian Andersen, The, by Signe Toksvig, 155
Literature of the Second Self, The, by C. F. Keppler, 155
London, 23, 43, 49, 94–106, 139

Macaulay, Rose, 153
Mackenzie, Compton, 153, 157
Macmillan, Sir Frederick, 116, 158
Macmillan, Harold, 48, 122, 141, 150
"Madame du Deffand" by Lytton Strachey, 52
Malamud, Bernard, 151
Mansfield, Katherine (Kathleen Beauchamp), 20, 21, 98, 100, 107, 136, 137, 138, 148, 158

Mark, Thomas, 68, 116, 123, 134, 149–50
Marlow ("Borlase's") School, 89
Marriott, Charles, 28, 52, 149
Marsh, Sir Edward, 149
Mary, Queen of Scots, 67, 131–32, 160
Maugham, W. Somerset, 18, 20, 109, 123–31, 134, 149, 159
Mayne, Ethel Colburn, 28, 149
Melchior, Lauritz, 19
Meredith, George, 27, 52, 110
Mersey Mission to Seamen, 139
Meynell, Viola, 153
Morris, William, 84
Motifs, various, 132–33, 140, 141–46
Mott, Frank Luther, 23–24
Murry, John Middleton, 20, 98, 148, 158
Mussolini, Benito, 63, 70, 71, 144

"Nail in the Coffin, The," by Alec Waugh, 159
Nevill, Lady Dorothy Walpole, 113
New Zealand, 28, 111, 145
Newton, Douglas, 74
Nicolson, Harold, 64
Novels, various: *Anthony Adverse* by Allen, 116; *Antic Hay* by Huxley, 107; *Barchester Towers* by Trollope, 91; *Barren Leaves* by Huxley, 107; *Between the Acts* by Woolf, 53; *The Brothers Karamazov* by Dostoevski, 55; *Cakes and Ale* by Maugham, 123–24, 134; *Christian* by Caine, 51; *The Column* by Marriott, 52; *Crime and Punishment* by Dostoevski, 78; *Crome Yellow* by Huxley, 107; *David Copperfield* by Dickens, 17, 51, 153; *Don Quixote* by Cervantes, 56, 102, 146; *The Dove's Nest* by Mansfield, 107; *Ethan Frome* by Wharton, 52, 127; *Forever Amber* by Winsor, 116; *Frankenstein* by Shelley, 110; *Futility* by Gerhardi, 156; *Gin and Bitters (The Full Circle)* by Mordaunt ("A. Riposte"), 129–30; *Gil*

Novels, various (*Cont.*)
Blas by Lesage, 108; *The Golden Bowl* by James, 52, 96; *Gone with the Wind* by Mitchell, 116; *The Great Gatsby* by Fitzgerald, 115; *The House on the Sands* by Marriott, 52; *The Hunchback of Notre Dame* by Hugo, 24; *If Winter Comes* by Hutchinson, 53; *Illusions Perdues* by Balzac, 51; *Jane Eyre* by Brontë, 81–82, 110; *Kronstadt* by Pemberton, 55; *The Longest Journey* by Forster, 52; *The Man of Property* by Galsworthy, 52; *Moll Flanders* by Defoe, 108; *Nicholas Nickleby* by Dickens, 35; *Northanger Abbey* by Austen, 118; *Nostromo* by Conrad, 71; *Of Human Bondage* by Maugham, 127; *Orlando* by Woolf, 127; *Pamela* by Richardson, 108; *Peregrine Pickle* by Smollett, 51; *The Plumed Serpent* by Lawrence, 107; *A Room with a View* by Forster, 51; *The Secret Agent* by Conrad, 51; *Sons and Lovers* by Lawrence, 44, 109; *The Sun Also Rises* by Hemingway, 115; *To the Lighthouse* by Woolf, 127; *Tom Jones* by Fielding, 51, 108; *The Turn of the Screw* by James, 98; *Two or Three Graces* by Huxley, 107; *Ulysses* by Joyce, 107; *Vanity Fair* by Thackeray, 51, 106; *The Waves* by Woolf, 140; *Where Angels Fear to Tread* by Forster, 51; *Wuthering Heights* by Brontë, 51; *The Years* by Woolf, 53

"Ode on Intimations of Immortality" by William Wordsworth, 80
Onions, Oliver, 153
Ouida (Louise de la Ramée), 110

"Pardoner's Tale, The," by Geoffrey Chaucer, 142
Pater, Walter, 110
Paul, David Blackwood, 111–12
Phelps, William Lyon, 91

Pickford, Mary, 19
Pippett, Roger, 124
Plays, various: *The Cathedral* by Box, 76–77; *A Comedy of Errors* by Shakespeare, 40; *Ghosts* by Ibsen, 43; *Kind Lady* by Chodorov and Haight, 160; *King Lear* by Shakespeare, 72; *Love in a Cottage* by Maugham, 159; *Love's Labour's Lost* by Shakespeare, 52; *A Man with Red Hair* by Levy, 157; *Murder in the Cathedral* by Eliot, 53, 85, 155, 157; *Night in the House (The Old Ladies)* by Ackland, 157; *Romeo and Juliet* by Shakespeare, 159; *The Tempest* by Shakespeare, 31–33, 51, 154
Poe, Edgar Allan, 27, 110, 136, 137
Polchester, 73–77, 84–91, 137
Polperro, Cornwall, 12, 87
Pound, Ezra, 64
Powell, Anthony, 151
Powell, William, 65
Prelude, The, by William Wordsworth, 79
Priestley, J. B., 153; as critic, 20, 109, 123, 147, 151; co-author of *Farthing Hall*, 40, 117–19, 123
Pritchett, V. S., 21, 131
Proust, Marcel, 52
Purdy, James, 151
"Pursued-Protagonist Pattern," 39–41, 60, 69, 70, 98–100, 101–2, 125, 131, 155

Queen Elizabeth I, 67, 131–32
Queen Victoria, 43, 74–75, 95–96, 107
Queen Victoria by Lytton Strachey, 107

Rank, Arthur, 154
Realism vs. Romanticism, 20, 26–27, 31, 48, 71, 99–100, 116–17, 118
Richardson, Dorothy, 20, 105, 109
Richardson, Samuel, 26–27, 108
Robinson, Edward G., 157
Romanticism, *see* Realism vs. Romanticism

Index

Rose (motif; flower and color), 145–46

Ruskin, John, 84

Russia, 18, 25, 49, 55–63, 66, 71, 97, 126–27, 136, 139, 156

Sadleir, Michael, 92–93

Sainte-Beuve, C. A., 107–8

Scott, Sir Walter, 17, 26, 108, 110, 143, 158

Secker, Martin, 18, 42

Selznick, David, 65, 159

Sensationalism, literary, 23–24

Shakespeare, William, 31–33, 40, 51, 52, 54, 72, 75, 154

Snow, C. P., 151

Somerset and All the Maughams by Robin Maugham, 159

Sontag, Susan, 148

Southey, Robert, 119

Sower Myre Farm, Cumberland, 140

Spencer, Elizabeth, 151

Starkie, Enid, 90

Steen, Marguerite, 11, 20, 47, 60, 78, 91, 98, 123, 133, 147, 154

Stein, Gertrude, 148

Stevenson, Robert Louis, 17, 26, 116

Strachey, Lytton, 20, 52, 107

Strong, L. A. G., 20, 107, 121, 147, 148

Swinnerton, Frank, 12, 20, 153

Temple, Shirley, 65

Thackeray, William Makepeace, 17, 18, 23, 51, 95, 105–6

Thompson, Francis, 79

Thorndike, Dame Sybil, 160

Tigers (motif), 144

Tolstoi, Count Leo, 112

Towers (motif), 143

Trollope, Anthony, 22, 23, 73, 91–93, 109, 143

Truro, Cornwall, 73, 87

Tunney, Gene, 19

Turgenev, Ivan, 55

Walpole, Dorothy (Dr. Dorothea; sister), 19, 26, 50

Walpole, George Henry Somerset (Bishop of Edinburgh; father), 18, 19–20, 31

Walpole, Henry (16th-century ancestor), 131

Walpole, Horace (fourth Earl of Orford), 17, 18, 23, 52, 118

Walpole, Hugh (*see also* Chronology in front): popularity during lifetime, 11, 17–22, 147–49; reputation since death, 17, 21–22, 147, 151–52; personality, 18, 19, 22–23, 50, 90, 108, 113, 149; travels, 18–19, 55–58, 63–64, 127, 131–32, 138, 140–41; education, 18, 19, 89, 139, 141, 161; childhood, 19, 26–27, 139, 154; sexual beliefs, 19–20, 24, 47, 69–70, 108, 151; as teacher, 19, 28, 34; physical descriptions of, 19, 112; as government worker, 58, 63, 139; as lecturer, 63, 92, 147, 149; as anti-intellectual, 106–13; as layman missionary, 139, 161; typical work habits of, 148–50

WRITINGS OF:

"The Abbey" (fragment), 27

Above the Dark Circus (Am.: *Above the Dark Tumult*), 40, 100–02, 126, 129, 146, 151

"Absalom Jay," 98, 138

"The Adventure of the Imaginative Child," 25

All Souls' Night, 136

And So—Victoria (screenplay; co-author?), 153

Anthony Trollope, 91–93, 107, 153

The Apple Trees, 139–40, 141

"Bachelors," 137

"Billy's Christmas Eve," 143

The Blind Man's House, 113–15, 141, 145

The Bright Pavilions, 67, 119, 120, 125, 131–34, 145, 151, 160

"The Brother," 137

Captain Nicholas, 64–66, 67, 68, 94, 103, 106, 114, 129, 131, 141, 144, 150

Walpole, Hugh (*Cont.*)
The Captives, 77, 80–82, 88, 94, 97, 142, 145, 151
"A Carnation for an Old Man," 138
The Cathedral (novel), 27, 42, 58, 73–77, 81, 82, 84, 86, 87, 88, 94, 139, 150, 153
The Cathedral (play), 76–77
"The Church in the Snow," 138
"The City Under Fire" (fragment), 158
"The Clocks," 143–44
"The Crabtree" (fragment), 158
"The Critic," 138
The Crystal Box, 139, 141
The Dark Forest, 25, 42, 55–58, 59, 60, 61, 70, 112, 141, 150
David Copperfield (screenplay; co-author Howard Estabrook), 17, 153
"The Dog and the Dragon," 138
"The Dove," 138
The Duchess of Wrexe, 24–25, 52, 55, 94, 95–96, 97, 104, 106, 126, 138, 142, 144, 149
"The Enemy," 137
The English Novel, 109
"The Exile," 137
"Fanny Close," 98
Farthing Hall (co-author J. B. Priestley), 40, 117–19, 121, 123, 145, 153
"Fear's Face," 27
"A Field with Five Trees," 142
Fortitude, 27, 42–45, 46, 48, 50, 51, 53–54, 55, 63, 69, 77, 83, 89, 95, 97, 112, 139, 142, 143, 151, 153
The Fortress, 40, 119, 123, 124–25, 126, 129, 131, 133, 143
"The German," 64
The Gods and Mr. Perrin (Am. version of *Mr. Perrin and Mr. Traill*), 25, 34–40, 150–51
The Golden Scarecrow, 77, 79–80, 88, 97, 145, 154, 160
"Green Courts" (fragment), 27, 155

The Green Mirror, 25, 55, 61–63, 65, 67, 76, 81, 94, 95, 97, 99, 122, 142–43, 149, 153
"Green Tie," 137
"Half-Way Upstairs," 138
Hans Frost, 42, 45–48, 50, 52, 62, 65, 68, 94, 106, 112, 116, 117, 127, 128, 143, 145, 150
Harmer John, 30, 84–85, 86, 87, 141, 145
"Harmer John: A Portrait," 157
Head in Green Bronze, 25, 136, 161
Herries series (*see also* individual titles), 18, 118–27, 131–35, 141, 151
"The Honey-Box," 138
A Hugh Walpole Anthology, 147, 161
The Inquisitor, 25, 40, 53, 73, 85–87, 88, 90, 94, 131, 139, 141, 155, 157
Jamaica Inn (screenplay; co-author?), 153
Jeremy, 25, 87, 88, 89, 112, 138, 142, 153
Jeremy and Hamlet, 25, 87, 88–89, 144, 151
Jeremy at Crale, 34, 87, 89
John Cornelius, 24, 42, 45, 48–50, 94, 106, 112, 130–31, 141, 143
Joseph Conrad, 71–72, 91, 93, 107, 153, 156
The Joyful Delaneys, 25, 40, 94, 102–3, 106, 112, 118, 131
Judith Paris, 25, 119, 120, 122–24, 125, 127, 129, 131, 145, 150
Juvenilia, 26–28, 116, 135, 138, 160
Katherine Christian, 119, 120, 134–35, 141, 145
The Killer and the Slain, 25, 40, 64, 66, 69–71, 102, 114, 137, 156
"Kim" (screenplay; not produced), 48, 153
A Letter to a Modern Novelist, 109

Little Lord Fauntleroy (screen-play), 48, 50, 153
"Lois Drake," 98
Maradick at Forty, 27, 30–33, 35, 40, 42–43, 47, 51, 62, 82–83, 97, 98, 99, 112, 118, 142, 143, 154
"Miss Morganhurst," 98
"The Monkaster Feast," 138, 160
Mr. Huffam, 136
Mr. Perrin and Mr. Traill, 33–40, 42, 44, 52, 56, 60, 95, 98, 112, 130, 138, 142, 149, 151, 154, 155
"Mrs. Porter and Miss Allen," 98
My Religious Experience, 161
The Old Ladies, 40, 89–91, 137, 145, 151, 158
"The Oldest Talland," 137, 138
Open Letter of an Optimist, 161
"Peter Westcott," 97, 98
Portrait of a Man with Red Hair, 82–84, 88, 90, 102, 118, 142, 143, 157
A Prayer for My Son, 64, 66–67, 114, 131, 145
"Preface," *The Waverley Pageant* (by Sir Walter Scott), eds. Walpole and Wilfred Parting-ton, 158
"A Prefatory 'Tale,'" *Famous Stories of Five Centuries,* eds. Walpole and Wilfred Parting-ton, 156
The Prelude to Adventure, 25, 42, 52, 77–79, 80, 88, 102, 126, 133
Reading: An Essay, 110–11, 139, 153
"Red Amber," 137
Robin's Father (co-author Rudolf Besier), 154
Rogue Herries, 24, 42, 58, 116, 117, 118, 119–22, 123, 124, 125, 127, 132, 134, 145, 150
Roman Fountain, 132, 138–39, 140–41, 160
"The Ruby Glass," 138, 145
"The Scarlet Fool," 27

The Sea Tower, 64, 66, 67–69, 70, 114, 115, 131, 143, 145
The Secret City, 25, 55, 58–61, 67, 70, 151, 161
"Service for the Blind," 141
Short stories (*see also* individual titles), 25, 27, 64, 79–80, 87–89, 97–98, 136–38, 141, 142, 143–44, 145, 157, 160, 161
"The Silver Mask," 138, 160
The Silver Thorn, 136
"Tarnhelm," 143
The Thirteen Travellers, 25, 97–98, 101, 106, 160
"Thirty Years a Novelist," 161
"The Tiger," 137, 144
"Troy Hanneton," 27–28, 42
"Turnip-Lanterns," 138
"Two Meredithian Heroines," 27
Vanessa (novel), 24, 119, 125–26, 131
Vanessa (screenplay; co-author Lenore Coffee), 153, 159
"The Whistle," 64
"The White Cat," 144
"William Somerset Maugham," 159
Wintersmoon, 42, 53, 94, 104–6, 109, 110, 115, 116, 117, 121, 122, 127, 143, 150
The Wooden Horse, 28–30, 41, 50, 51, 63, 65, 98, 112, 140, 142, 149, 154
The Young Enchanted, 31, 40, 94, 98–100, 105–6, 112, 118, 138, 143, 149, 151
Walpole, Mildred Barham (mother), 18, 19, 20, 88
Walpole, Robert Henry ("Robin"; brother), 19, 27
Waste Land, The, by T. S. Eliot, 107
Wells, H. G., 19, 21, 34, 139
West, Rebecca, 21, 100, 105, 148
Wilson, A. C., 83
Woolf, Leonard, 109
Woolf, Virginia, 64; as New Novel-ist, 11, 17, 18, 20, 21, 54, 108–9, 147, 148; as critic, 20, 21, 153;

Woolf, Virginia (*Cont.*)
  as friend, 21, 116, 127, 145, 149; on and in *Hans Frost*, 48, 116, 145; *The Years* and *Wintersmoon*, 53; satirized in *Young Enchanted*, 100; Walpole analyzes, 100, 108–9; and husband, Leonard, commission *Letter to a Modern Novelist*, 109; Walpole calls "a darling," 116; as writing model, 116, 127, 149; *To the Lighthouse*, 127; *Orlando*, 127; *The Waves* quoted, 140; and *Apple Trees*, 140; as "Jane Rose," 145; on *Green Mirror*, 153

Wordsworth, William, 79, 80, 119

Wynn, Keenan, 160

"Younger Generation, The," by Henry James, 20, 95, 147